Totem Salmon

"House is a marvelous explainer of how things are and how they work and how, if you grasp the puzzle presented by . . . a native species of salmon, you might better understand yourself." BARRY BLAKE, *North Coast Journal*

"A marvelously vivid and thoughtful book."
California Coast and Ocean

"This graceful book is a welcome gift." *Coast Weekend*

"Reading [House's] words, I feel I am returning to my own native element: rain flavored with cedar and the exact stone recipe that thrills me home. If a salmon can find clues this subtle, what are we not seeing yet?"
KIM STAFFORD, *The Sunday Oregonian*

"Here is the quintessential deep ecology book, with no mention of the controversial and ambiguous term."
KEN OTTER, *Deep Ecology News*

"*Totem Salmon*, a lyrical meditation about place, binds together two epic journeys: one about humans, one about fish."
MICHAEL BLACK, *San Francisco Examiner-Chronicle*

"A landmark work of environmental activism."
CHRISTOPHER CAMUTO, *Audubon*

"Freeman House masterfully narrates the daily challenges that he and his cohorts have faced in trying to bring back a once almost extinct native Chinook salmon run, and places it all within a larger cultural and historical context."
MIKE HELM, *Express Books, East Bay Express*

"Inspired and well-written . . . a terrific introduction to an ethic called 'bioregionalism.'" *Publishers Weekly*

"I know of no book that is as local as House's and no book that is more global in its implications."
JONAH RASKIN, *Santa Rosa Press Democrat*

Totem Salmon

LIFE LESSONS FROM ANOTHER SPECIES

FREEMAN HOUSE

BEACON PRESS · BOSTON

BEACON PRESS
25 Beacon Street
Boston, Massachusetts 02108-2892
www.beacon.org

Beacon Press books are published under the auspices of
the Unitarian Universalist Association of Congregations.

05 04 03 02 01 00   9 8 7 6 5 4 3

This book is printed on totally chlorine free (TCF) paper that meets the
uncoated paper ANSI / NISO specifications for permanence as revised in 1992.

Text design by Christopher Kuntze
Composition by Wilsted & Taylor Publishing Services

LIBRARY OF CONGRESS CATALOGING-IN-PUBLICATION DATA
House, Freeman.
    Totem salmon : life lessons from another species / Freeman House.
      p.   cm.
    ISBN 0-8070-8548-0 (cloth)
    ISBN 0-8070-8549-9 (pbk.)
    1. Salmon.   I. Title.
    QL638.S2H68   1999
    597.5'6—dc21   98-37308

To Nina

And in grateful memory
of the life and work of
Nat Bingham

What better agents than ourselves to revive our region's salmon runs? We are the natural kith to their kin. We marvel at the miracle of their return, argue over their health, and rise early to troll and mooch for them in the dark, testy water of the North Pacific. We ceremoniously savor their firm yet delicate flesh, subtly cooked in a myriad of local and family recipes. In spices, smokes, and sauces, salmon is the soul food of the North Pacific. And while they delight our senses, the salmon also represent us in a profound and heartfelt way. They are the precious mettle of our watersheds. They embody our home places. Salmon are the deep note of our dwelling here, the silver soul of this green bell—steelhead, sockeye, coho, chum, pinks, and kings.

TOM JAY, *"Homecoming"*

CONTENTS

people like Doug Aberley, David Abram, Peter Berg, Jim Dodge, Jeremiah Gorsline, David Haenke, Tom Jay, Dolores LaChapelle, Jerry Martien, David McCloskey, Stephanie Mills, Judith and Christopher Plant, David Simpson, Whitney Smith, Gary Snyder, Victoria Stockley, Lee Swenson, and George Tukel. Certainly this book would not have been written had I not been exposed to their luminous minds.

I also am indebted to the life-changing books of Paul Shepard, Thomas Berry, and Raymond Dasmann, among many others.

Editors Deanne Urmy and Chris Kochansky have gentled me through many a tight spot. They have taught me more than they know. Working with such talented people is one of the few unambivalent pleasures to be found in writing.

Mickey Dulas, Ali Freedlund, Verna Jigour, Jerry Martien, Sarah Pollock, Vicky Pollock, Willow Rain, David Simpson, Whitney Smith, Rondal Snodgrass, and Charlie Solo have each read parts of the manuscript and offered useful advice and encouragement. Seth Zuckerman helped me by reviewing the entire text, and by his steady friendship.

It takes a long time to write a book—longer than I thought, longer than the patient people at Beacon Press thought—and I deeply appreciate the generous assistance provided by the Deep Ecology Foundation and the Sitka Institute. Professor Ted Bernard had the courage to put my name forward for the Rufus Putnam Visiting Professorship at Ohio University, and I remember warmly the rich time that honor provided. Ted and his wife, Donna, and Meg and Bill Hummons provided me with hospitality in Athens, Ohio; Lisa Faithorn and Jann Hoffman in Walnut Creek, California; Carolyn Severid and Dorik Mechau, Richard and Nita Nelson, Jan and John Straley in Sitka, Alaska. Thank you all for taking me into your homes and feeding me and for giving me a glimpse of your places through your eyes.

Although this book is dedicated to my life partner, Nina Blasenheim, no library of books could compensate for the friendship, moral and material support, and reality checks with which she has blessed me.

The thought that this book might somehow lighten the grave responsibilities my children will inherit has almost, but not quite, assuaged my guilt at being something less than a whole parent while I was writing. So a last word to my son Daniel, my daughter Laurel, and my stepdaughter Angeline: You were never as far from my thoughts as I may have sometimes caused you to think. Be attentive; listen to what the planet is saying; it's alive, all of it.

1 · IN SALMON'S WATER

*Sometimes your storyline is
the only line you have to Earth.*

SHARON DOUBIAGO

J AM ALONE in a sixteen-foot trailer by the side of a river. It is New Year's Eve, 1982. The door to the banged-up rig stands open, and when the radio is off I can hear water in the river splashing endlessly over cobbles. The oven is on full blast. Its door hangs open too. The heat rises to the ceiling in layers, ending at the level of my chest. My face is hot, but my ankles and knees are cold and damp. On the radio the Grateful Dead and fifteen thousand celebrants woozily greet the new year at the Oakland Coliseum. Ken Nordine's deep beatnik baritone drones on. Ken Kesey babbles. Any moment now, Bill Graham, undressed as Baby Time, will be lowered from the rafters. The band lurches through the music, loses the thread entirely, and after a long time finds it again, the beat loose and insouciant throughout. The band seems to say, "See? Told you we could find it again." It all makes sense with enough LSD, I suppose, and I have sometimes lived my life as the Grateful Dead plays its music, drifting in and out of the right way to be, risking everything on

I

an exploratory riff. But tonight I am focused and full of purpose. My only drug is a poorboy of red port, which I sip cautiously.

I turn the radio off and listen. Then, to hear better, I turn the lights off too. I am listening to the water. If you listen carelessly, the water in a rushing river sounds like a single thing with a great fullness about it. But when you begin to try to sort out the sound of one thing *within* the sound of the water, the moving water breaks into a thousand different sounds, some of which are in the water and some of which are in your mind. Individual boulders rolling along the bottom. The Beatles singing *ya-na-na-na*. The one sound breaks itself into separate strands that intertwine with each other like threads in a twisted rope. Some strands are abandoned as new ones are introduced, making a strange and hypnotic music. Listening to running water is a quick route to voluntary hallucination.

Among the many voices of the water, I am trying to distinguish the sound of a king salmon struggling upstream. It is a foolish undertaking and it never works. I hear a hundred fish for every one that is actually there, and then miss the one that is. The only sure way to locate a fish in this realm of sensation is to walk to the river's edge and play your light along the surface of the water where it passes through the weir. The king salmon may be large or small, it may weigh three pounds or thirty. If it has swum into the pen above the weir, I will pull the long latchstring that releases the gate that closes the mouth of the weir, so the fish can go neither upstream nor down. This doesn't happen very often in 1982.

A little more than three years ago, a state fisheries biologist told us that this race of native king salmon is done for. I am still not totally sure he wasn't right. The state Department of Fish and Game is spread thin. They can't afford to expend their scarce resources on a river that has next to no hope of continuing to produce marketable salmon for a diminishing fishing fleet. But a small number of residents of the remote little valley have not been able to bring themselves to stand by and watch while one more race of salmon disappears, especially the one in the river that runs through their lives. They have begun with little idea of what can be done. They've talked to other people like themselves, and also to ranchers, loggers, academic biologists, and commercial fishers. They have read books and sent away for obscure technical papers. They've developed a scheme that they hope will enhance the success of the spawning of the wild fish. Through stubborn persistence they've convinced the state to let them have a go at it.

By the last night of 1982, this little group has grown into a cohort of several dozen residents who are spending a great deal of time trying to forge a new sort of relationship to the living processes of their home place. We also have learned to deal with bureaucracies outside that place, and we have incorporated as the Mattole Watershed Salmon Support Group. We have raised money. We have entered into contracts. We are inventing our strategies as we go along.

I am part of that cohort. I am tending a weir with an enclosed pen behind it that is meant to capture wild salmon in order to fertilize and incubate their eggs. I am working by myself, which is unusual. Normally a crew of two or three would share these long nights. Most often, David and/or Gary, two of the people who initiated the effort, would be here. But it's a holiday. Everyone else has pressing engagements. The fish, however, know nothing of holidays. The spawning season is almost over, and we few who care for the salmon haven't come anywhere close to reaching the goals we have set for ourselves this year.

(Now, nearly twenty years later, we find ourselves with lots of company—hundreds in our own watershed and thousands in other places all over North America—and I write out of curiosity as to what motivated people, myself included, to act in such a way. It is my hope that by the time you close this book we will both have some of the answers.)

The weir looks like fish weirs have always looked on this coast, a fence angled upstream across the river from either bank at enough of a bias against the current so that it will not offer more resistance than it can endure. It closes off passage upstream except through a one-foot opening at its apex. In earlier times, a fisher with a net or spear might have stood behind or above the opening. For our purposes, the opening serves as the doorway to a trap, or to a pen. Although built from materials manufactured elsewhere, it has a funky look; it blends in. Panels of redwood one-by-one, grape stakes in another life, are spaced at one-inch intervals horizontally and lashed to metal fence posts pounded into the river bottom. Each panel has a chickenwire apron attached at its bottom. The aprons are held to the bottom by sandbags, gravelbags really, each one weighing about forty pounds. Filling and hauling the bags two at a time takes up most of the two-hour drill required for three or four people to install the temporary structure.

The salmon's progress upstream is one of many marvels of the salmonid life cycle. The grace and strength required to overcome waterfalls and other blockages, the stamina to endure floodwaters, the systematic persistence necessary to thread the maze that a big logjam presents—these are attributes so wondrous that we must consider them in the same realm as the mysterious intelligence that allows the creature to distinguish between the smell of her particular natal stream and the smell of the rest of the world of water. But when the fish swims into an enclosure that requires her to seek an exit *downstream*, she becomes slow and seemingly confused. It will usually take her some hours to discover the downstream exit that she found so quickly before, when it was the passage upstream. Her slow meanders seem now to lack purpose; escape from the trap, when it comes, seems almost accidental. It is as if nothing matters now that the path to the spawning gravels is blocked.

I had argued with my coworkers that we should take advantage of this weakness. We humans have little enough advantage dealing with such a marvelously functional aquatic creature, and I am a person who loves his sleep. Salmon have yet to recognize that we are trying to help them; they continue to evade us. We are social workers whose clients decline to be served. Use our terrestrial, linear intelligence, I said, to fashion traps that would hold the fish until morning. Wait to handle them until after a second cup of coffee.[1] And we had, for two years, fashioned beautiful traps to stand at the mouth of the weir. The traps had been built from the same grape stakes as the weir panels, and they had cleverly hinged plywood covers opening out from either side of the top. A three-quarter-inch cable slung all the way across the river from the top of the gorge at either side allowed a running block to be installed. Another line running through the block attached the traps to a hand-operated winch for installing the heavy hulks of the things in their exact locations, or for pulling them out quickly when the level and velocity of the rising water threatened to tear them apart or sweep them away.

But there was something about the traps—the sound that the waters made passing through so much enclosure, or perhaps the shadow that the things cast in the liquid boil below—that seemed to prevent the fish from entering. We had observed fish moving at dusk work their way right up to the mouth of a trap and then, in an instant, turn and disappear downstream. When they did enter and stayed for the night, they leaped against the plywood covers looking for a way out, wounding themselves and threatening their precious manifest of unfertilized eggs. Such a trap was too obviously a construct in service of human comfort, and we were, after all, seeking to serve the ends of the other species. Thus we have switched to a system featuring the larger and less secure pen, and the alarm clock set at two-hour intervals, and the muddled brains of the attendants.

If the salmon are running in the deep night in December or January, it is likely that the moon is new, that the river is rising, and that the water is clouded with silt. It is probably raining. The salmon will use these elements of obscurity to hide them from predators while they make a dash toward the spawning grounds.

Tonight it is drizzling lightly, the air full of water only just heavy enough to fall to the ground. The drops cut across the beam of my headlamp and seem to be held there motionless, a black-and-white cartoon of rain. In the circle at the end of the beam, the black shag of redwood, and the huckleberry understory is everywhere weighted down with water and dripping.

I am in clumsy chestwaders that weigh seven or eight pounds. The rubber boot-legs join at the crotch and the garment continues up to just above the sternum, where it's held in place by a pair of short suspenders. The suspenders are never adjusted correctly; they are inevitably too tight or too loose. I lurch about like a puppet with too few moveable joints. Long-johns top and bottom against the cold. A Helly-

and wait. I continue to hear the sound for a period of time for which I have no measure . . . and then it stops. I wait and wait. I hold my breath but do not hear the sound again. There is a long piece of parachute cord tied to a slipknot that holds open the gate at the mouth of the weir. I yank on the cord and the gate falls closed, its crash muted as the rush of water pushes it the last few inches tight against the body of the weir.

And now that I am no longer trying to sort one sound from another in the sound of the water, it is as if the water has become silent. It is dark. If the world were a movie, this would be cut to black. When I hear the sound I am waiting for, it is unmistakable: the sound of a full-grown salmon leaping wholly out of the water and twisting back into it. My straining senses slow down the sound so that each of its parts can be heard separately. A hiss, barely perceptible, as the fish muscles itself right out of its living medium; a silence like a dozen monks pausing too long between the strophes of a chant as the creature arcs through the dangerous air; a crash as of a basketball going through a plate glass window as he or she returns to the velvet embrace of the water; and then a thousand tiny bells struck once only as the shards of water fall and the surface of the stream regains its viscous integrity.

I flick on my headlamp and the whole backwater pool seems to leap toward me. The silver streak that crosses the enclosure in an instant is a flash of lightning within my skull, one which heals the wound that has separated me from this moment—from any moment. The encounter is so perfectly complex, timeless, and reciprocal that it takes on an objective reality of its own. I am able to walk around it as if it were a block of carved stone. If my feelings could be reduced to a chemical formula, the experience would be a clear solution made up of equal parts of dumb wonder and clean exhilaration, colored through with a sense of abiding dread. I could write a book about it.

The coevolution of humans and salmon on the North Pacific Rim fades into antiquity so completely that it is difficult to imagine a first encounter between the two species. Salmon probably arrived first. Their presence can be understood as one of the necessary preconditions for human settlement. Pacific salmon species became differentiated from their Atlantic ancestors no more than half a million years ago.[2] Such adaptations were a response to their separation from their Atlantic salmon parent stock by land bridges such as the one that has periodically spanned the Bering Strait. By the time the Bering Sea land bridge last emerged, twelve thousand to twenty-five thousand years ago, in the Pleistocene epoch, the six species of Pacific salmon had arrived at their present characteristics and had attained their distribution over the vast areas of the North Pacific. As the ice pack retreated, the species continued to adapt ever more exactly as stocks or races—each finely attuned to one of the new rivers and to recently arrived human predators. If indeed humans first arrived in North America after crossing that land bridge from Asia, the sight of salmon pushing up the rivers of this eastern shore would have served as proof that this place too was livable.

On this mindblown midnight in the Mattole I could be any human at any time during the last few millennia, stunned by the lavish design of nature. The knowledge of the continuous presence of salmon in this river allows me to know myself for a moment as an expression of the continuity of human residence in this valley. Gone for a moment is my uncomfortable identity as part of a recently arrived race of invaders with doubtful title to the land; this encounter is one between species, human and salmonid. Such encounters have been happening as long as anyone can remember: the fish arrive to feed us and they do so at the same time every year and they do so with an obvious sense of intention. They come at intervals to feed us. They are very beautiful. What if they stopped coming?—which they must if we fail to relearn how to celebrate the true nature of the relationship.

For most of us, the understanding of how it might have been to live in a lavish system of natural provision is dim and may be obscured further by the scholarship that informs us. Our understanding of biology has been formulated during a time of less diversity and abundance in nature; our sense of relationship is replaced by fear of scarcity. By the time the anthropologists Alfred Kroeber[3] and Erna Gunther[4] were collecting their impressions of the life of the Native Americans of the Pacific Northwest, early in the twentieth century, the great salmon runs that had been an integral part of that life had already been systematically reduced. It may be this factor that makes the rituals described in their published papers seem transcendent and remote: ceremonial behavior that had evolved during a long period of dynamic balance has become difficult to understand in the period of swift decline that has followed.

It seems that in this part of the world, salmon have always been experienced by humans very directly as food, and food as relationship: the Yurok word for salmon, *nepu*, means "that which is eaten"; for the Ainu, the indigenous people of Hokkaido Island, the word is *shipe,* meaning "the real thing we eat." Given the abundance and regularity of the provision, one can imagine a relationship perceived as being between the feeder and those fed rather than between hunted and hunter. Villages in earlier times were located on the banks of streams, at the confluence of tributaries, because that is where the food delivers itself. The food swims up the stream each year at much the same time and gives itself, alive and generous.

It is not difficult to capture a salmon for food. My own first memory of salmon is of my father dressed for work as a radio dispatcher, standing on the low check dam across the Sacramento River at Redding and catching a king salmon in his arms, almost accidentally. The great Shasta Dam, which when completed would deny salmon access to the headwaters of the river, was still under construction. Twenty years later, as an urbanized young man, I found myself standing with a pitchfork, barefooted, in an inland tributary of the Klamath River, California's second largest river system. The salmon were beating their way upstream in the shallow water between my legs. Almost blindly, my comrades and I speared four or five of them. When the salmon come up the river, they come as food and they come as gift.

Salmon were also experienced as *connection*. At the time of year when the salmon come back, drawn up the rivers by spring freshets or fall rains, everyone in the old villages must have gained a renewal of their immediate personal knowledge of why the village was located where it was, of how tightly the lives of the people were tied to the lives of the salmon. The nets and drying racks were mended and ready. Everyone had a role to play in the great flood of natural provision that followed. The salmon runs were the largest annual events for the village community. The overarching abundance of salmon—their sheer numbers—is difficult to imagine from our vantage point in the late twentieth century. Nineteenth-century firsthand accounts consistently describe rivers filled from bank to bank with ascending salmon: "You could walk across the rivers on their backs!" In the memory of my neighbor Russell Chambers, an octogenarian, there are stories of horses refusing to cross the Mattole in the fall because the river had for a time become a torrent of squirming, flashing, silvery salmon light.

It is equally difficult to imagine a collective life informed

and infused by the exuberant seasonal pulses of surrounding
nature over a lifetime, over the lifetime of generations. But
for most of the years in tribal memory of this region's original inhabitants, the arrival of salmon punctuated, at least
once annually, a flow of provision that included acorn and ab-
alone in the south, clams and berries and smelt in the north,
venison and mussels and tender greens everywhere. Humans
lived on the northwest coasts of North America for thousands of years in a state of lavish natural provision inseparable
from any concept of individual or community life and survival. Human consciousness organized the collective experience as an unbroken field of being: there is no separation
between people and the multitudinous expressions of place
manifested as food.

But each annual cycle is punctuated also by winter and
the hungry time of early spring, and in the memory of each
generation there are larger discontinuities of famine and upheaval. Within the memory of anyone's grandmother's
grandfather, there is a catastrophe that has broken the cycle
of abundance and brought hard times. California has periodic droughts that have lasted as long as a human generation. And there are cycles that have longer swings than can
be encompassed by individual human lifetimes. Within any
hundred-year period, floods alter the very structure of rivers. Along the Cascadian subduction zone, which stretches
from Vancouver Island to Cape Mendocino in California,
earthquakes and tidal waves three to five hundred years apart
change the very nature of the landscape along its entire
length.[5] Whole new terraces rise up out of the sea in one
place; the land drops away thirty feet in another. Rivers find
new channels, and the salmon become lost for a time.

Even larger cycles include those long fluctuations of temperature in the air and water which every ten or twenty thou-

sand years capture the water of the world in glaciers and the ice caps. Continents are scoured, mountain valleys deepened, coastlines reconfigured, human histories interrupted. These events become myths of a landscape in a state of perpetual creation; they are a part of every winter's storytelling. The stories cast a shadow on the psyche and they carry advice which cannot be ignored. Be attentive. Watch your step. Everything's alive and moving.

On a scale equivalent to that of the changes caused by ice ages and continental drift are the forces set loose by recent European invasions and conquests of North America, the exponential explosion of human population that drives this history, and the aberrant denial of the processes of interdependence which has come to define human behavior during this period.

Somewhere between these conflicting states of wonder—between natural provision erotic in its profligacy and cruel in its sometimes sudden and total withdrawal—lies the origins of the old ways. Somewhere beyond our modern notions of religion and regulation but partaking of both, human engagement with salmon—and the rest of the natural world—has been marked by behavior that is respectful, participatory, and ceremonial. And it is in this way that most of the human species has behaved most of the time it has been on the planet.

King salmon and I are together in the water. The basic bone-felt nature of this encounter never changes, even though I have spent parts of a lifetime seeking the meeting and puzzling over its meaning, trying to find for myself the right place in it. It is a *large* experience, and it has never failed to contain these elements, at once separate and combined: empty-minded awe; an uneasiness about my own active role

both as a person and as a creature of my species; and a looming existential dread that sometimes attains the physicality of
a lump in the throat, a knot in the abdomen, a constriction
around the temples. They seem important, these various elements of response, like basic conditions of existence. I am
smack in the middle of the beautiful off-handed description
of our field of being that once flew up from my friend David
Abram's mouth: that we are many sets of eyes staring out at
each other from the same living body. For the instant, there
is a part of that living body which is a cold wet darkness containing a pure burst of salmon muscle and intelligence, and
containing also a clumsy human pursuing the ghost of a relationship.

    I have left the big dip net leaning against the trailer up
above the river. I forget that the captured fish is probably confused and will not quickly find its way out of the river pen. I
race up the steep bank of the gorge as if everything depends
upon my speed. My wader boots, half a size too large, catch
on a tree root and I am thrown on my face in the mud. The
bank is steep and I hit the ground before my body expects to,
and with less force. I am so happy to be unhurt that I giggle
absurdly. Why, tonight, am I acting like a hunter? All my
training, social and intellectual, as well as my genetic predis-
position, moves me to act like a predator rather than a grateful, careful guest at Gaia's table. Why am I acting as if this is
an encounter that has a winner and a loser, even though I am
perfectly aware that the goal of the encounter is to keep the
fish alive?

    I retrieve the dip net and return more slowly down the
dark bank to the river. Flashing the beam of my headlamp on
the water in the enclosure, I can see a shape darker than the
dark water. The shape rolls as it turns to flash the pale belly.
The fish is large—three or maybe four years old. It seems as
long as my leg.

Several lengths of large PVC pipe are strewn along the edge of the river, half in the water and half out. These sections of heavy white or aquamarine tubing, eight, ten, and twelve inches in diameter, have been cut to length to provide temporary holding for a salmon of any of the various sizes that might arrive: the more closely contained the captured creature, the less it will thrash about and do injury to itself. I remove from the largest tube the perforated Plexiglas end-plate held in place by large cotter pins.

I wade into the watery pen. Nowhere is the water deeper than my knees; the trap site has been selected for the rare regularity of its bottom and for its gentle gradient. The pen is small enough so that anywhere I stand I dominate half its area. Here, within miles of its headwaters, the river is no more than thirty feet across. The pen encloses half its width. I wade slowly back and forth to get a sense of the fish's speed and strength. This one seems to be a female, recently arrived. When she swims between my feet I can see the gentle swollen curve from gill to tail where her three to five thousand eggs are carried. She explores this new barrier to her upstream migration powerfully and methodically, surging from one side of the enclosure to another. Using the handle of the net to balance myself against the current, I find the edge of the pen farthest from the shore, turn off the headlamp, and stand quietly, listening again.

The rain has stopped. Occasionally I can hear her dorsal fin tear the surface of the water. After a few minutes I point my headlamp downward and flick the switch. Again the surface of the water seems to leap toward me. The fish is irritated or frightened by the light, and each of her exploratory surges moves her farther away from me, closer to the shore.

The great strength of her thrusts pushes her into water that is shallower than the depth of her body and she flounders. Her tail seeks purchase where there is none and beats the shallow water like a fibrillating heart. The whole weight of the river seems to tear against my legs as I take the few steps toward her. I reach over her with the net so that she lies between me and the mesh hoop. I hold the net stationary and kick at the water near her tail; she twists away from me and into the net. Now I can twist the mouth of the net up toward the air and she is completely encircled by the two-inch mesh. I move her toward deeper water and rest.

There are sparks of light rotating behind my eyes. The struggle in the net translates up my arms like low-voltage electricity. The weight of the fish amplified by the length of the net's handle is too much. I use two hands to grasp the aluminum rim at either side of the mouth of the net, and I rest and breathe. After a bit, I can release one side of the frame and hold the whole net jammed against my leg with one hand. I reach for the PVC tube and position its open mouth where I want it, half submerged and with the opening pointing toward us. I move the net and the fish around to my left side and grasp through the net the narrow part of her body just forward of her tail—the peduncle—where she is still twice the thickness of my wrist.

I only have enough strength to turn the fish in one direction or another; were I to try and lift her out of the water against her powerful lateral thrashing, I would surely drop her. The fish is all one long muscle from head to tail, and that muscle is longer, and stronger, than any muscle I can bring to bear. I direct her head toward the tube, and enclose tube and fish within the net. I drop the handle of the net, and move the fish forward, toward the tube.

There is a moment while I am holding the salmon and mesh entwined in elbow-deep water when everything goes still. Her eyes are utterly devoid of expression. Her gills pump and relax, pump and relax, measured and calmly reg-

ular. There is in that reflex an essence of aquatic crea-
turehood, a reality to itself entire. And there is a sense of
great peacefulness, as when watching the rise and fall of a
sleeping lover's chest. When I loosen my grasp, she swims
out of the net and into the small enclosure.

Quickly, trembling, I lift the tail end of the tube so that
her head is facing down into the river. I slide the Plexiglas
endplate into place and fasten it, and she lies quietly, the tube
just submerged and tethered to a stout willow. I sit down beside the dark and noisy river, beside the captured female
salmon. I am sweating inside my rubber gear. The rain has
begun again. I think about the new year and the promise of
the eggs inside her. I am surrounded by ghosts that rise off
the river like scant fog.

His sickness was only part of something larger, and his cure would be found only in something great and inclusive of everything.

LESLIE MARMON SILKO, *Ceremony*

THE AMPUTEE can occasionally feel the ghost of a sensation that seems to come from the place where the lost limb once was. The arm or leg, foot or finger is gone, and so are its functions, but the nervous system does not immediately adjust to the loss. For a long time after the trauma, the amputee may feel signals from the absent limb: feelings of warmth or cold, twinges, the painful numbness of the limb gone to sleep.

Each creature, each organism, has some functional role in the web of life out of which it has emerged. The local field of being that we call the ecosystem must experience a period of adjustment when one of its organisms has disappeared— even if the disappearance has occurred over a period of time beyond human understanding. When people, accidentally or purposefully, experience engagement with these fields of being, the direct, ineffable sense of the ghosts of lost creatures may come visiting.

These ghosts are globes of emptiness floating throug‍‍ bloodstream of life, nearly lost memories of the void left by some absent life form. Ecosystem absences can become a palpable presence, a weird stillness moving against the winds of existence and leaving a waveform of perturbation behind. Most humans are slower to see and feel in this realm, surrounded as we are by the noise of machinery, the buzz and hum of electricity. We need a tsunami of absence to get our attention. But on a dark night by a river, the noise of which is a form of silence, such a ghost may find a voice in the human imagination, and when a place is full of ghosts, the search for peace of mind can fill up with such perturbations.

So powerful are the ties between humans and salmon that even in rivers and streams where salmon are still running—but in numbers severely diminished—the ghosts of salmon are rising. Salmon resides in the hearts of humans: for many, even the imminence of its absence creates an active ghost. All over northwest North America, races of salmon exquisitely adapted to specific rivers, or forks of rivers, or smaller tributary creeks, have been lost. The American Fisheries Society documents that 214 such populations had been extirpated as of 1991 on the Pacific coast of the United States alone.[1] Tonight, by the side of the river, one of those ghosts, perhaps the ghost of the Bear Creek king salmon from just over the ridgeline, has found its way through my ears or through my eyes or my fingertips to lodge itself in the muscles at the base of my neck. I am trying to explain why I am here while the rest of the world seems to be elsewhere drinking champagne breakfasts.

Twice more on the first morning of the second year of Ronald Reagan's first term I set a bedside alarm and scramble down the banks to inspect the weir. I see no more fish. When

I reawaken at ten in the morning, the weak storm of the night before has moved inland and we are in an area between fronts that is full of tentative sunlight and mild breezes, suggestions that there is a condition other than winter. The little weather radio is switched on directly after the burner under the coffee water is lit: *Occasional showers today. A new low-pressure system is positioned offshore and will bring rain tonight, heavy at times, north of Shelter Cove.*

Shelter Cove is due west. Where I am, I cannot know how such a forecast will effect my situation. It is often the case that storms stray from the tidy areas the forecasters have designated for them, and "Rain, heavy at times" is a frequently used phrase on the weather radio this winter. It means prepare for the worst. The smell of mold is strong in the trailer this morning.

After a breakfast of crackers and cheese and coffee, I remove a panel from the weir so that in the unlikely event that a salmon moves upstream in the daylight she or he will pass on by. This relieves me of the need to check the pen during the day and maintains an element of randomness in our relationship. I move to the upstream side of the weir to inspect the female who joined us last night, and the two males in separate tubes that we have been holding for several days waiting for a mate or mates.

One of the males is large, approaching thirty pounds. His nose has grown the hook that identifies the male salmon after a period in fresh water, there are white abrasions on his head and tail, and his appearance in general has grown dark and deteriorated. Salmon don't eat once in fresh water, and their flesh softens as it provides the only nutrients available for the last rush upstream. The other male is small, perhaps fourteen inches long, a two-year-old "chub" or "jack," a bright fish without the distorted nose and tail of his elder. These younger fish arrive at the forefront of the run every year. Most of them are males, and they precede the older fish upstream and wait.

All three fish are lying quietly, sheltered from the glare of the bright January morning in their temporary housing. I roll up my sleeves and remove the endplate from the rear of the female's tube, then tip the tube up toward me slightly. She makes a swimming motion, a slow languorous wave that travels from head to tail. I reach my hand into the tube, running my palm and fingers lightly along her belly. She doesn't react to my touch. The cold water desensitizes my hand; it is as if there is a quarter-inch of insulation between my fingertips and the rubbery band of muscle that protects her belly. My rolled sleeve touches the water and wicks cold wetness up to my elbow.

The eggs this female is carrying began to form before she entered the river. As she approached the headwaters they grew and individuated and ripened, four thousand potentials for new salmon, all within a membrane that holds them together in a solid mass. I am stroking the belly of the captured fish to determine how close she is to depositing her eggs in the river gravel, ready for fertilization by one of the restive males. If the eggs are approaching ripeness, the skein that holds them together will be stretched close to disintegration and the individual eggs will begin to roll free of each other. At optimum ripeness, I will be able—gently, gently—to squeeze a single egg out through her vent. Not yet, not today. Today the eggs cling to each other, clustered worlds in a soft galaxy. I am diffident, clumsy; my wooden fingers ignorant and apologetic.

The open weir gives me the freedom to survey the stream above and below it, looking for those who have gotten past the fence and those who have not yet arrived. Wandering on

the river in thin winter light, we are sometimes called upon
to engage a mystery. To say that the conditions under which
salmon reproduce are difficult is to understate the obvious.
If I were to see angels cavorting in the wind, I would find it
no more difficult to comprehend than the way salmon reproduction is carried forward in the rushing water.

Precocious male chubs arrive first and wait, a wave of
reproductive insurance. They are fertile and as ready as any
human adolescent, but later the larger males will attempt to
exclude them from the final intimacy. The three- and four-
and sometimes five-year-old males arrive next, darker and
more damaged than their smaller, brighter brothers. They
have grown downturned snouts with snaggled teeth. Noses
and tails have been abraded white as the heavy fish leaped upstream against rock and waterfall; in some places white fun-
gus grows on the sores. The two age classes avoid each other.
None of the fish have eaten since entering fresh water and
each individual seems all nerves and attitude. Alternately
edgy and languid, they patrol the pools and the dark spaces
beneath the bushes that grow on the banks. Should a larger
fish encounter a smaller one, there is a sudden stir: the larger
fish will lunge and butt and snap to discipline and chase away
the smaller.

The females arrive individually, all purpose and system
and sleek intent. Each one of them is searching for a certain
configuration of gravel and current that will serve her needs.
The gravel must be of a certain size—the size of a small man's
fist, say—the water of a depth adequate to float the fish during the work to come. By the time she has traveled this far
upstream, there is an imperative apparent in her movements: she is feeling the pressure of the season; timing is all.
She ignores predators and works in broad daylight, in bright
water.

She powers up against the current over a reach of attractive spawning gravel and drifts back. She powers up again, more slowly now, and seems to inspect the gravel with her nose. She is looking for the place where she will build the nest—the redd—the home of the future of the race. The water is a foot or more deep, with enough velocity and gradient to have carried the smaller cobbles on past. Her muscular tail, strengthened by the long sea journey, abraded and scarred by the struggle upstream, still contains strength enough to move half a yard of gravel, a few cobbles at a time. With the leverage of her whole body behind a turn, a swipe of the tail turns up a rock or two. A cloud of silt drifts downstream and disappears. She turns on her side and slaps the loosened cobbles with her tail—a double-time cadence faster than the palpitating heart of the human witness and loud enough to be heard over the sound of the water, loud enough to be heard by the bears and raccoons that lurk at the river's edge each year at this time. She will dig until there is a depression up to fifteen inches deep in the river's bottom.

Language seems inadequate to describe what follows. I have never been able to separate out the dance of the fish from my own bedazzled perception. (And I doubt that fish dance, if we consider dance as a formalized series of movements separate and different from other forms of movement.) I hold my breath, as if to breathe would upset some balance, would shunt some spermatozoon off its track. I am a grateful participant in the process I am witnessing, but a participant who doesn't understand the *function* of his participation. This void of purpose and understanding, coupled with my total absorption in the act of creation, may be as close as I ever get to an experience of nonhuman nature. For a moment, the separation of mind that seems to define the human experience is gone—or at least it has retreated to an obsequious, secondary position.

The behavior exhibited by salmon in the act of procreation is often described as courtship, a metaphor that has always struck me as lazy and inadequate. The vernacular sense of the word describes an attempt to win over, a systematic flirtation. It also describes a choice: one is struck with desire for a particular other and applies oneself to winning that other's admiration. Look to an etymological dictionary, however, and another, richer interpretation of the word emerges. The word *court* originates as a noun, and it refers to an enclosed space. The enclosure was originally most likely a wall, but it could as easily be the space between the banks of a stream. By extension, the word has also come to mean those beings assembled in the space—"a crowd of attendants or company of soldiers" in my dictionary, but in our context a little galaxy of creatures and relationships. The word *cohort* comes from the same root. If you were to turn *cohort* into a verb, you might have a description of a group of beings constrained to a place and seeking a means to dance out their relationships within and to that space. Cohorts give expression and meaning to the place that contains them. Another definition of the word is "associate" or "accomplice," and this describes a male and female salmon's relationship more accurately than a word implying flirtation. But none of these words fit what happens next.

The female is completing her nest, the redd. As she digs she concentrates on deepening it at the center, building an ovipository, a pocket nest for the protection of her eggs. She may have been at this for hours now, or even days. The male up to this point has shown limited interest. He may drift through the area of activity—especially if another male is showing interest—but he has been of no help in moving rocks. But now the female begins to act like a worker testing the result of her labors to see how close to completion it is.

Arching her body, she probes the bottom of the depression with her tail, drifts to the surface of the running water, and probes again.

Once she is satisfied, she hovers over the redd with her vent over the nest pocket. Her lower jaw drops open; the resistance of the gaping mouth helps her to hold herself in place in the current. While the female has been probing, the male has begun to hover steadily nearby, and he has begun to tremble. Now it seems as if an invisible soupy fog of piscine eroticism rises off the water and envelops the observer. The fog is a dense, cold, quiet mixture of sex, death, and inevitability.

A single male will join the female in the nest, quivering now more noticeably. As the two of them turn and turn again to race the length of the redd, the male will frequently cross over the back of the female to swim at her other side; thus the temptation to call the act a "courtship" or "dance." Other males will hover at the periphery of the action. When they come too close, the dominant male makes threatening moves out of the circle toward the intruders. The young jacks turn and flee, but the older, heavier males retreat only slightly, hardly turning out of the way. The tension is thick, palpable.

After a time, some signal passes between the two principals that the female is ready. Side by side, both are now holding their jaws agape to steady themselves against the current. The female's tail is arched down toward the pocket at the bottom of the nest. Both are now trembling with the effort and with the gravity of the moment. The male releases a cloud of milt, milky and sperm-filled. At the same instant, the female releases a portion of her eggs. Often, and nearly faster than the eye can see, one or two other males dash over the scene and add their milt to the mix. For a moment, a milky cloud fills the pool. Another moment and it has washed away downstream. If we are lucky, we will have caught a glimpse of the eggs drifting down, slow comets dimly seen through a dense and fertile fog. Immediately, the female will move upstream of the redd and begin to cover the eggs.

The first few motions of her tail will dislodge no gravel, but will serve to create a current that distributes the eggs more widely between the sheltering interstices of the rocks. Then, with increasing vigor, she will move enough gravel to cover the eggs. The finished nest will be difficult to distinguish from the surrounding bottom of the stream, except that the gravel is cleaner and it may mound up slightly where the eggs are incubating. The nearby depression created in covering the eggs will likely serve as the beginning of the next nest.

Now the process begins again. One of the benefits of carrying thousands of potential embryos is that not all must be risked in a single location. Most female king salmon build three or four redds before they have completed their cycle.

Then silence. The progenitor fish, male and female, will drift to shelter, get caught against logs or rocks they no longer have the energy to avoid, and begin to die, a process that may take hours or days. Their efforts have left them wounded and raw, and expanses of flesh have been worn away by the female's gravel-moving work. The secondary males will move on, perhaps to find other opportunities before their time is up. Females stay to protect their nests against predators until they have no energy left.

Eagles, bears, raccoons, and otters have been patrolling the edges of the streams throughout the entire cycle; they feast and feast and feast. In this way a multitude of salmon bodies, carrying nutrients gained thousands of miles away in the depths of the sea, are carried away from the edge of the stream where they will also contribute (and contribute importantly) to the health and fecundity of the forest floor. Those carcasses that decompose in the water will feed microorganisms that will later feed salmonid offspring.

That should be enough. Even if the ghost of salmon hasn't found you before now, the experience of the invisible cloud full of absolutes rising off the living water at the moment of creation may be enough to claim your life, or at least a small part of it, in service to that creation forever.

Once, during a time when I was working as a salmon fisher on a cannery-owned boat in southeastern Alaska, I took a walk by myself up into the mountains above Ketchikan. My wandering took me to the edge of a small lake where someone had left a little skiff at the edge of the water, not in good repair, but still fit enough to float. One oar was missing, but the single oar allowed me to paddle out into the center of the lake. The boat leaked badly and I stopped to bail, using a rusty coffee can left in the bottom. After a while I paused, looked up, enjoyed the sight of the snow-covered peaks looming above the tops of the large old hemlocks and red cedars on the surrounding shore. Then, for no particular reason, I looked down into the water, and I could not understand what I was seeing.

The water was clear and shallow, and the entire bottom below me was a brilliant red—a red somewhere between crimson and orange—and it moved, writhing and undulating in a way that was terrifying. It was one of those temporary rifts in reality, when it seems you have suddenly stepped into a world of which you have had no experience or expectation or memory. It's a rift that happens most often in dreams. The color was beautiful but the way it moved was frightening. It was as if the earth had been gashed or badly scraped along the bottom of the lake and the wound was welling blood. Then, just as quickly, I realized what I was seeing. The bottom of the little lake was covered with sockeye salmon in their spawning colors, brilliant blood-red bodies with bright olive-green heads. They were engaged in the reproductive rite of their species, and I had just happened to glance down and become a witness. All at once I was wrapped around by the miracle of natural provision in all its profligate abundance. What a welcome the planet has laid out for us! How easy to gather from its bounty what we need to survive! And I understood at the same moment, free-falling and abandoned, how bereft, how orphaned from its sources of sustenance my own species has become.

That memory will be twenty-one years old this August, old enough to buy a drink in California, and it lives in my imagination as freshly as if it had occurred this afternoon: the exuberance, the crushing sadness. I am still explaining to you why I am here on this river in mid-winter.

Experiences like these, and a few good teachers, have taught me to trust and love my senses as pathways to reality. Civilization creates for me a thousand other worlds that have little to do with my senses, a thousand illusions among which to choose. It is one of the functions of much of contemporary education and politics to convince me that my choices are limited to these creations. Were there a television in my home, it would spend twenty-four hours a day convincing me that life is either a series of dangers and disasters or an endless series of shallow and banal encounters with uninteresting people. Magazines and newspapers tell me the same story. Shopping malls connected by broad paved highways are filled with objects presented as the rewards of existence—the flesh of the world converted to doodads. Big Science has had a good deal to do with the creation of this deadly alternative reality, and science has willingly lent its hand to the great effort to convince me that the evidence of my senses and the intuitions that arise from their use are illusory.

But there is a scientific practice that precedes Big Science, a devotion to patient and scrupulous observation of the world and its creatures. I have come to love this discipline, now known as natural history, which delves ever more deeply into the physiological and behavioral differences between my species and others. There is an explosion of this kind of knowledge accumulating in our era, driven by an increasing awareness that many species are disappearing and that we know desperately little about them and therefore little about how to save them. As part of the effort, technicians in lab smocks have isolated salmon eggs and sperm under laboratory conditions and have observed the process of their union minutely and repeatedly, so that I am able to know what follows my observation at the redd.[2]

By the time the egg released by the female has drifted through the cloud of milt to reach the bottom of the stream, fertilization will have occurred or not occurred. At the moment the egg is exposed to water, its fragile, nearly invisible shell begins to expand slightly and to harden. The single entrance by which the male's sperm will achieve its access, a funnel-shaped, pinprick-sized opening called a micropyle, begins to close. This process happens quickly, and by the time the egg reaches the bottom of the stream the opportunity for conception has passed. The male milt has by this time drifted downstream, out of play, in any event.

Until the male releases the milt, the mature sperm cells have been inert. Once they hit the water over the redd they become ferociously active, stimulated by the presence of

coelemic fluid, the substance that has lubricated and separated the eggs inside the female. The eggs now also exude a
second chemical, which helps guide the sperm to the micropyle. In a matter of seconds the sperm wakes to its moment
of purpose, seeks out its goal, and achieves union within the
egg—all in swiftly moving water. It is little wonder that the
success rate of fertilization in the most pristine of habitats
hovers at less than 50 percent.[3]

The process is awesome, place-perfect, a jewel of local evolution in response to the ever-changing conditions in
this single tiny Pacific drainage over a span of tens of thousands of years. The Bear River, which enters the sea directly
north of the Mattole, has lost its salmon, perhaps a human
generation ago. On the river north of that one, the mighty
Eel, king salmon arrive a month earlier than they do on the
Mattole, but in ever decreasing numbers. Travel south from
here, and you will cross several coastal streams of the same
order of magnitude as the Mattole. Some of them have supported king salmon populations in the past; none of them do
so now. Some two hundred miles south you will reach the
mouth of San Francisco Bay, which is fed by the confluence of
the great Sacramento and San Joaquin Rivers. This enormous hydrological system drains the Sierra Nevada and has
formed the Central Valley of California. It has always provided the largest range of salmon habitat in California, and
in the past it supported several stocks of native salmon. Now
the few native king salmon that race through the Golden
Gate each year have earned the dubious honor of becoming
representatives of the first such stocks to make it onto the endangered species list.

It is part of the grand evolutionary strategy of diversity
that different salmon stocks have evolved subtle but "hard-

wired" genetic differences as they have adapted to thousands of particular waterways as their reproductive homes. Each remaining native stock becomes increasingly precious: to use Gregory Bateson's famous line in a different context, these are differences that make a difference.

The Mattole River is small enough and so remote that the California Department of Fish and Game has never introduced hatchery-bred king salmon into it, as it has done in most of California's salmon streams. The Mattole stock is, in fact, one of the six or seven native king salmon stocks in California that has never been homogenized through interbreeding with hatchery fish, which might have their genetic origins almost anywhere. This makes the Mattole king salmon nearly unique as one of the southernmost native stocks in existence on the entire North Pacific coast. Any population's viability is most fragile at the furthest extension of its range, and the two-hundred-mile blank spot in the range of the king salmon population as a whole has torn a very large hole in California's coastal life zone, and in its economic outlook as well. The Mattole's is the stock most likely to provide strays that might successfully recolonize nearby coastal streams to the north and to the south when and if those streams recover their potential as reproductive habitats.

These were some of the arguments that we who fought to preserve the Mattole salmon used to dislodge the bureaucratic inertia that resisted our ambitions in the beginning, and they remain the reasons—the rational ones, anyway—that I find myself spending New Year's Eve and New Year's Day away from home in a damp and uncomfortable trailer.

Nothing in nature mimics a road.

DANNY HAGEN

DURING THE SALMONS' spawning work, the gravels
that cover the eggs are moved twice and any fine sediments
that might have been clinging to them are tumbled off. The
freshly tidied rocks are irregularly shaped and the interstices
between them provide shelter from predators and free passage of water through the loosened gravel bed. The oxygen
that is essential to the growth of the fetus will be drawn
from the water. As the fetus develops within the egg, its need
for oxygen will increase; it is critical to its survival that the
free passage of water through the redd not be restricted by
the accumulation of fine sediments. The process of nest-
building and fertilization, already honed to a fine edge by
evolution, will be for naught if the fertilized eggs are smoth-
ered.

Fifty years ago there was a better chance than there is now
that water would flow freely through a salmon redd for the
forty to sixty days it will take for the fish to hatch out. At

present, too many reaches of spawning habitat, already limited by requirements that the gravel be the right size and the water flow just right, have been compacted with fine sediments. To understand how this came to be, a short description of the processes of erosion and the human practices that accelerate them is useful.

When we glance at a stream in passing, we see it as it is in the moment; we tend to experience its channel as a static setting for the sight and sound of running water that we find so soothing. But over time the hydraulic processes of a stream channel are as dynamic as anything in nature. Streams are constantly cutting their way down through hills and mountains that have risen up in their paths in the past and are rising still. Each wet season, each and every rivulet and stream reconfigures itself.

The ability of a watercourse to move things in its path increases exponentially in proportion to its volume. Double the volume of water and its power to move things—its erosive or cutting force—increases by a factor of four; the quantity of material that can be carried increases by thirty-two; the size of the particle that can be carried increases by sixty-four. Winter flows can rearrange the largest rocks on a stream's bottom; they redistribute the trees and rootwads that have fallen into their path; they gouge out whole sections of streambank, along with the trees and brush growing there.

In spite of the large energies of this seasonal activity—and because of them—most streams, as they mature, reach a state of relative equilibrium with the landscape through which they flow. Ultimately they will find channels of harder bedrock that erode more slowly. The most erosive flows at the outside edge of a meander will encounter an outcropping that stabilizes that meander for a while. Gravity eventually dictates that streambanks will find an angle of repose that allows vegetation to grow root systems large enough to hold those banks in place for long periods of time.

The parts of the trees and shrubs that grow above ground will act as sieves and filters during flood times; they slow the water at the edges of the channel so that sediments and debris can drop out there to make soil for more vegetation. As vegetation takes hold on the edges of the stream, the flow of water is crowded toward the center, flushing the finer sediments out of the center of the stream. Depending on the volume and velocity of the flow, larger rocks and cobbles will settle out here and there to buffer the erosive forces at the bottom. In the flatter reaches of the stream, new gravels will be recruited behind accumulations of woody debris. If the gradients are just right, the new gravels will be of a good size for new salmon spawning habitat while the finer sediments continue to be swept on by. As the water tumbles over the temporary check dam created by a fallen tree, it scours out pools which newly emerged salmon fry will use in the earliest stages of their lives. They will hide from predators behind the bubble curtain of turbulence; they will feed on the larvae of insects that use the rotting wood.

As the stream, perhaps large enough now to be called a river, reaches its confluence with the sea, the gentler gradients slow its flow, and ever finer particles fall to the bottom. The finest of these will continue on downriver, back to the sea from which they have come. On average, and without mechanical disturbance of the surrounding hillsides by humans, a stream will after a time tend to erode no more soil in the short term than it can carry to the sea. This is so even in the newest and most active watersheds in North America, those of the Pacific Coast.

In the King Range, which forms the western side of the Mattole watershed, this process of maintaining equilibrium is of a larger magnitude than in most places, because these mountains are rising up out of the Pacific at a greater rate of speed than any others in North America. This is due to the King Range's proximity to the Triple Junction, a meeting of the Pacific, North American, and Gorda tectonic plates. The North American plate is moving steadily across the Pacific plate, and, in the process, grinding up the smaller Gorda plate. The King Range is that part of the North American plate that is bucking upward in bumps and jolts—at the rate of fourteen feet or so every thousand years—as the Pacific plate dives beneath it. The rock of the King Range, and of the Pacific Coast ranges in general, is no more than compressed material from the sea bottom—sandstones and shales that flake and erode easily under the force of flowing water.

The entire range of North Pacific salmon is coterminous with this "ring of fire," so called because of the tumult and upheaval, the fine network of earthquake faults and periodic volcanic eruptions that define the active geology of all the landforms surrounding the Pacific, the Peaceful Sea. Certain conditions are just a little more exaggerated at the Triple Junction.

Here there is plenty of water to do the work of erosion. Although Kings Peak is at the moment only 4,088 feet high, it and the peaks nearby rise higher than the hills of the Coast Range to the north and south of it. Thus the King Range creates what is known as an orographic effect, meaning that its higher elevations form the first landfall for powerful, fast-moving storms coming in off the Pacific. These storms sweep unchallenged over several thousand miles of open sea, growing larger as they go, and when they strike the peaks of the

King Range, they release enormous amounts of water. Honeydew, the closest settlement with an official gauging station inland of Kings Peak, is recorded as the wettest place in California. Wilder Ridge, which lies between Honeydew and Kings Peak, can receive half again as much rainfall as Honeydew, and winters measuring 100 to 150 inches of precipitation are not unusual. Thus the sediment load of the Mattole and the neighboring Eel River are rated as the highest in North America.[1]

In effect, the King Range is being washed down into the sea at very nearly the same rate it is rising up. A visiting geologist who worked with our salmon group for a few years searched out the figures for the rate of uplift extrapolated from core samples taken in the continental shelf just offshore of Kings Peak. He did some quick calculations and estimated that if it were not for this "background" erosion, Kings Peak would stand 40,000 feet high, half again the elevation of Mount Everest, rather than its current 4,000 feet plus.

Even though it moves so much material each year, the Mattole had tended toward a general state of equilibrium before the advent of roads and other bulldozed construction. The word *mattole* is said to mean "clear water" in the native language. And in the past the entire river system might become opaque with mud after a large storm. But in a matter of hours its tributaries would become clear again, and in a matter of days the main stem of the river would once again be bright water: *Mattole*.

The secrets of watershed equilibrium are not to be found so much in the splashing streams as on the hillsides above them. When the great rains fall, they distribute themselves more or less equally over the local landscape, which in the case of the rapidly rising King Range has arranged itself into a tortured asymmetry of steep slopes and narrow canyons. The soils that have had time to form on these slopes support a wide range of dense vegetation: chaparral on the highlands and on the hot southern slopes, a rich mix of Douglas-fir and hardwoods on the cooler slopes. Here and there, in the highlands, big sugar pines, trees more often found in the Sierras to the east; in the headwaters, which receive more fog, the grandeur of redwoods.

The streambanks themselves are held in place by a riparian community of willow and alder with a scattering of large and stately bigleaf maple and California bay laurel. These trees and shrubs themselves suck up an appreciable amount of the water that falls around them, but more importantly, their intertwined root masses hold the soil in place against the forces of gravity and erosion. It takes several storms each rainy season to saturate the sponge-like soil, after which the waters begin to seep and flow into a network of swales and depressions, thousands upon thousands of them.

Draw a diagram of the patterns of water on the wet slopes and they resemble nothing so much as the capillaries in our own bodies that deliver blood to every inch of skin surface. But in the case of the mountain, the flow is not up and out to the periphery but down and in to the heart of the sea. Gravity. The millions of acre-feet of water that fall on the slopes of the King Range are delivered to streams at the canyon bottoms in slow trickles that combine to form first and then second order tributary creeks, each of which has found its own armored bottom over time.

It is an elegant delivery system, evolved from a combination of biotic and geologic processes to mediate the tremendous erosive forces of the sea of water that falls on these hills most years. Where the system is undisturbed, water is distributed to the streams carrying a minimum of the silts and sediments that make up the rich soil above. I once walked through the bottom of Bull Creek Canyon in the Humboldt Redwoods State Park—where the original condition of the landscape can be experienced just a few miles northeast of the area I am describing—at the tail end of a storm that had delivered five inches of rain in a day. A score of streamlets were delivering water from the undisturbed slopes above in volumes large enough to overwhelm the culverts that had been installed beneath the paved road on which I walked. The water that was beginning to flow across the road was crystal clear.

While the tendency of the whole watershed as it matures is toward a state of equilibrium, its internal processes are in constant flux; changes occur when the microdrainages are disturbed in such a way as to combine their volumes or to divert them onto slopes that are not armored. The delicate equation that has defined the equilibrium of any microdrainage is altered when the volume of water moving through it is increased significantly. Such disturbances can occur whether or not there is human participation. An animal trail between microdrainages may be worn in over time at just the right gradient that it begins to divert water from one capillary to another. Periodic wildfires ignited by lightning may take out the vegetation holding the surface of a mountainside together. Landslides may follow that can divert the whole of a tributary stream. The new volumes of water may wash enormous amounts of soil and cobble into the system, and it might take five or twenty or a hundred years for the subdrainage to regain its stability, but the larger hydraulic system tends to maintain its elegant balance. Over time, the ability of the river system to transport the new sediments out to sea is increased in direct proportion to the volume of water that has scoured them into the system in the first place.

Enter the new human technologies that made possible the Douglas-fir logging boom of the 1950s and 1960s throughout the Pacific Northwest, technologies which gave humans the power to imitate a whole geological age in a mere twenty years. After the development of huge track-driven earthmovers, a spin-off from the armored tanks of World War II, we gained the capability to push miles of new roads across steep terrain which had previously thwarted access to the suddenly valuable trees. We could now mount kidney-jarring machines of a size and horsepower that made it seem as if we could compete with gravity. But this is a game that gravity always wins.

Most of the road-building was for the purpose of driving trailers heavily loaded with logs out of the woods and to the mills, which were usually many miles away. The heavily laden trucks did not do well on grades of more than 20 percent, so the roads were cut laterally across the steeper slopes, switching back and forth as they inched up or down a mountain. The notch cut laterally across the gradient to provide a flat surface for trucks is called a bench cut. The width of the flat surface is doubled when the materials cut out of the hillside are perched on its downhill edge, compacted enough by the weight of a Caterpillar tractor to make a solid surface, at least for a single season of hauling. Come winter, these Caterpillar constructs could become arteries of destruction.

Any single mile of raw new road notched out of a steep hillside might cut directly across dozens of capillary drainages, combining their flows into an inboard ditch that became in effect a new streambed, digging a channel two or four or ten feet deep in a single winter. Ever-larger volumes of water in the ditches increased until they either exploded through a too-sharp curve in the road, taking the roadcut with it, or were dumped through the occasional culvert onto unarmored banks. Culverts were made of corrugated steel and were expensive; the larger their diameter the more they cost.

The operators of the new machines were working in unfamiliar terrain (the tractor drivers almost always came from somewhere else), and they designed the roads as they went along. The design process—if we can call it that—was driven as much by the capabilities of the machines, the exigencies of the terrain and the moment, and the size of the operator's hangover, as it was by any understanding of the hydrologic processes it was altering. Driven by the giddiness of quick profits, the roadbuilders used as few culverts as possible, and when culverts were used, the volume of water they would need to carry in these wettest of California winters was inevitably underestimated. The undersized tubes of steel often clogged with debris the very first winter after their installation, creating a blowout that might carry thousands of yards of shattered material into the drainage below.

The new roads, numerous as they were, still only delivered the sawyers to the general proximity of the thousands of trees it was their charge to take out. In the service of efficiency, the cut trees had to be stockpiled somewhere so that the log trucks and their drivers would not be kept waiting. This required yet another machine with tracks, a loader large enough to heft the huge boles onto the trucks. The log deck and the turning radius of the loader in turn created the need for periodic flat landings the size of baseball diamonds, and so even larger amounts of fill were pushed to perch precariously on the steep slopes. These landings tended to become saturated quickly in the winter following the initial operation, and that material, too, could collapse and pour into the streams at the bottoms of the canyons.

The same machines that cut the roads were equipped with

a winch and a short spool of cable on their stern ends. From the landings, rough skid trails could be pushed up the slope. Once a tree was felled by a sawyer, the dozer could be turned around, the cable extended, and the bole of the tree dragged down toward the landing. As it was pulled down the slope, each tree gouged out a shallow gully, creating channels that delivered yet more water to saturate the landings below. These gullies cut deeper as the winters passed, creating dendritic patterns of mineral subsoil. More and more topsoil was in the river, killing fish, rather than on the slopes where it might sprout new trees. Often, to save time and money, the logs were hauled right down the center of the channels of tributary creeks, tearing up the cobble armoring the bottom of the streams and ripping out the stream-side vegetation.

The logging boom that had begun no earlier than 1947 was still gaining momentum when a so-called hundred-year storm hit the California coast in the winter of 1955, the year I graduated from high school. There is no way to estimate how many millions of yards of soil and rock poured into the river system that wet winter; no one was counting. But a rough estimate of the combined effect of logging operations and that storm on the river system can be gained by a quick comparison of aerial photos of the river drainage. Such photos have been taken every five years, on average, since 1942, when a large-scale air-photo inventory was begun as part of the war effort.

In the 1942 photos, it is difficult to even find the river in the dark sea of trees, so dense is its riparian overstory, so narrowly is its deep channel contained. Only in the lowest five miles of the channel does it begin to broaden out and become visible. A few dairy farms dot the alluvial plain near the river's mouth. The 1960 photos, however, show the river as a

shallow braided channel picking and repicking its way
through a cobbled floodplain that is many times the width of
its summer flow. The grassy farms, along with their homes,
barns, and outbuildings, have disappeared, replaced by cobble that glares starkly in the black-and-white photos: the
dense riparian shade has been torn away by the great flood of
water and the debris it carried with it. Old-timers along the
lower river remember whole log decks showing up, scattered in yards once the flood waters receded—yards that had
once sat a half-mile back from the river.

The disaster of 1955 did little to slow the momentum of
the logging boom. During the late fifties and early sixties,
three sawmills were working around the clock in the lower
valley and still could not handle the volume of timber that
was coming out of the mountains. So many log trucks were
coming in and out of the valley that the drivers, in a rare instance of cooperative planning, had agreed to use one route
into the valley and another on the way out, so that traffic
wouldn't be slowed on the narrow, winding roads. Another
"hundred-year" flood hit only nine years later, when a monstrous rain melted the snowpack in the higher elevations in a
matter of hours.

In 1973, the logging boom was slowed by the adop-
tion of the Z'berg-Nejedly Forest Practice Act, which instituted a uniform code for timber harvest practices in the
state of California—after most of the largest trees had been
taken. In theory, licensed professional foresters were now
held responsible for agency-approved designs for roads that
would cause the least damage to the watershed. But in practice operators were inclined to embrace the old theorem that
the shortest distance between two points is a straight line.
Before the Forest Practice Act, no one had been required

to replant behind the clear-cuts that industrial foresters had begun to prescribe in the sixties. The new rules still sanctioned clear-cutting, but now regenerative replanting was required.

By this time, more than 80 percent of the old-growth trees had been taken out. Whole mountainsides that had been shaded by large old conifers were now grown up with brush species, and abandoned roads patterned the slopes like lace. In 1983, crossings and culverts long abandoned were still collapsing into the waterways. The rootwads that had continued to hold the slopes in place for an additional twenty to twenty-five years after the trees had been cut were now rotted away; as the roots rotted, the structural integrity of the slopes was undermined, and they collapsed in massive landslides.

The elegant equilibrium of watershed processes had been drastically disturbed, and that equilibrium had played an essential role in providing salmon with their reproductive habitat. The huge winter flows were no longer adequate to the challenge of maintaining equilibrium in the hydraulic system. Their ability to carry the annual sediment load out to sea had been overwhelmed by the enormous amounts of rock and mud and organic debris that had been added to the load. The deep channels and pools of the mainstream of the river filled up with debris. The rushing water spread laterally, ripping out the stream-side vegetation that had previously cooled and crowded it into a single deep channel. Tributary streams, with their smaller volumes of water, were often clogged at their confluence with the mainstream by logjams, which collected nearly impermeable accumulations of mud and rock behind them. In some places, the larger volume of water in the main stem cut down through its own new bedload over a period of years, leaving the mouths of some tributaries perched a dozen or more feet above their confluence with the river, preventing the up-stream migration of salmon in whole subdrainages.

In the mainstream, islands of cobble and mud built up in mid-channel, further diminishing the power of the flow by forcing it into a braided configuration that rearranged itself again and again each winter. Salmon searching for spawning gravels would have found them in a new location each year, if they found them at all. The spawning migration begins at the start of each rainy season, and, likely as not, the erratic flow patterns later in the year—in the two-month period during which the eggs are incubating in the gravel—might choke the eggs in the new redds with fine sediments. The redds might be buried two to ten feet deep by a constantly shifting bedload, or the braided channels would reconfigure themselves in such a way as to leave the redds high and dry.

By the early 1980s, the river system had already been working for twenty years to reestablish its pre-bulldozer equilibrium, and it was obvious to the most minimally in-formed observer that the work would not be finished any time soon. So large were the volumes of debris introduced into the aquatic system in the twenty-five-year period of the unregulated logging boom that it would take the river many years more to move them through the system. Even with the significantly improved land-use practices introduced with the new forest practice rules of 1973, it was obvious that the process of readjustment we were witnessing was going to take longer than we were going to live—quite likely longer than our children were going to live, should they find the means to stay here and watch.

In the interim, what would happen to the runs of native

king and silver salmon who were dependent on the equilibrium between the rising mountains and the roaring waters? These were questions the Mattole Salmon Group and
the soon-to-emerge Mattole Restoration Council would attempt to address.

The wind from the south has picked up—a sure indication of a full-fledged winter storm—and it is blowing
stinging rain into my face and down behind the collar of my
raincoat. At this time of year, when the soils are saturated,
any little rain can turn into a deluge that will bring the
streams up to bank-full stage in a matter of hours. Depending
on the volume of water the storm is carrying, these are the
times when we stand our best chance of capturing salmon.
In late December and early January, we are seeking the last
of the fish whose freshwater run began in November. As the
streams rise and become more turbid, the fish will move out
of their shelters in the deep holes and under submerged logs.
The higher flows will give them the water they need to work
their way over the obstacles posed by logjams and rockfalls;
the mud in the water will hide them from predators. If the
water rises slowly enough, we may have time to capture one
or two of these swimmers.

It's always a temptation to leave the weir in the water as
long as we can on the rising flow. But before the streams have
filled their channels, our pen and weir must be out of the
water or be washed away. The weir panels are small, to make
them easy to handle by one person. It takes two hours to
build a single panel and it requires a dozen or more of them
to span the river and create an enclosure. If we lose them to
the river, we lose twenty-four hours of careful construction.
More than once, having waited too long, we have spent additional hours searching the reaches of the river downstream

for the ruined pieces of the weir, hoping perhaps to salvage a panel or two.

Now the river beside me is already beginning to cloud up with silty runoff. I'm guessing that it's approaching noon already, no more than five hours of light remaining. It's clear by now that the trap will need to be taken out of the river today and that I'm going to need to find help to do it. But Gary Peterson, the fisheries biologist the salmon group has lured out of his masters program at Humboldt State University, has gone to the same Grateful Dead Concert that helped me stay awake last night: it's a matter of spiritual practice, something you can't argue with. And David Simpson, whose dogged energy holds this and several other efforts together, is at a rare family reunion in Lake Tahoe, an occasion such a family-oriented man could not deny. I don't know if Sandy or Judi or Gene or Ray—fishers and homesteaders who live within a half-hour's drive—are at home.

When I reach camp, though, Richard Gienger's big old van is idling near the trailer. The truck is idling because its starter motor is out. I know this because Richard, who lives with his family and their goats only a couple of miles up the road, drops by the trap several times a day whenever the truck is working. His bright hazel eyes and wide smile are like lights in the dark tangle of his long black hair and full beard. He is slouched in the doorway of the trailer holding the last of the coffee steaming in my cup.

I am aware that while Richard may be standing in the door of the trailer, he is most likely thinking of several other places he might better be. He is a leader in the struggle to save the Sinkyone Wilderness, on the coast just south of the Mattole. The back of his truck is full of boxes of completed survey forms that are the basic building blocks of a comprehensive overview of the use of the Mattole by salmonids. I know, too, that these boxes full of paper should have been turned into a readable document a month ago. Richard is probably wondering if his pioneering streambank stabilization work on a tributary of the neighboring Eel River is holding together. Today, like every day, Richard will be trying to be everywhere at once. He is grinning broadly; he has seen the newly captured salmon.

Soon after he and his family settled in the Mattole, in 1969, Richard experienced an epiphany. One day he stood on a bridge over the Mattole and watched a large male king salmon, deep in the chest and longer than his arm, swim lazily beneath him. The river is narrow and shallow this close to its headwaters; the monstrous size of the fish was all out of proportion to the daintiness of the picture-book stream. Although the fish could not have been more than four or five years old, its languorous, comfortable movements seemed to Richard to be an expression of thousands of years of dominion in these waters. The salmon *belonged* in the landscape in a way that Richard could hardly imagine himself or his peers belonging.

When you come into a country that has been radically altered by recent human use, it is difficult to extrapolate the earlier condition of the landscape from what you can see around you. Who could imagine the rich complexity of a forest, for instance, when the only point of reference is a recent clear-cut? Most people don't think to try. What possible benefit could be realized from the study of how the land once was? Sometime during the first few years of Richard's residence in the Mattole, a few copies of anthropologist Gladys Ayer Nomland's 1935 monograph *Sinkyone Notes* showed up in the tiny Briceland store. The rare pamphlet soon sold out, as Richard and a few others searched it for clues to the nature of the place and how earlier peoples had lived here. If we could undo the web of life in such a short time, there might be a way, some dreamed, to participate in some sort of re-weaving of the web within a similar span of time. One of Nomland's informants, Sally Bell, had died barely half a century ago. She had died less than a mile from Richard's home.

Nomland's monograph told of "first salmon" ceremonies and claimed that the people who were called the Sinkyone were the southernmost practitioners of this type of self-regulatory observance, some variation of which can be found all the way north to Alaska, and on around the Pacific Rim to Kamchatka and Hokkaido. It told of "first acorn" ceremonies, shared with many California tribes, and of a ritual relationship to deer and deer meat that informed every aspect of life. It told of the speech the "shaman" would make at the beginning of the annual world renewal ceremony: "Nagai-cho made this world and patted it down so everything would stay in place. But bad men were not satisfied and tore it down, tore up the ocean banks, tore up the trees, tore down the mountains. Since that time, we have had to sing and dance every year to make it right again."[2]

It was clear to Richard that there was no road back to a preindustrial relationship to place. Who would want it? Machines and other technologies have become part of the modern human psyche and social fabric, he realized; there is no turning back. However many bloody and soil-encrusted skills in self-reliance recent settlers like himself had accumulated, there were few indeed among them who could imagine making it without their twenty-year-old pickup or their beat-up third-hand chain saw. After four or five generations of the combustion engine, the skills it took to survive without gasoline seemed as remote as the alembic of any medieval alchemist.

But perhaps there were signposts that led forward to a different set of relationships among lives in what had come to be called, since the early seventies, the *post*industrial age.

After a few seasons of roaming the woods, after ten years of experiencing just how little was necessary for survival (a discovery that put him well over at least one of our rigid late-twentieth-century mental boundaries), new notions of human identity began to form in Richard's heart. This is how he sees it now.

It doesn't take an expert in the manipulation of statistics to understand that the survival of the entire human species depends on a sustainable relationship to the local expression of the processes of the biosphere. From everything one can learn through the nearly impenetrable veil of modern history, prehistoric humans acted out this latter assumption for most of our species' time on Earth. The very roots of the word *indigenous* mean "of a place." But the seductive social mechanics of the relatively recent Industrial Revolution have been so successful that even as we humans have exhausted our sources of sustenance, we have convinced ourselves that there is no other way to act. We have engaged in a process of purposeful and systematic forgetting; we have lost previous models of a more elegantly balanced life among humans, and we have convinced each other that it is fruitlessly utopian to imagine any other way of life.

Richard began to wonder what he could do to "make things right," to regain the proper human role as a functional and benign part of the landscape surrounding us. He yearned for a relationship resembling the voluptuous comfort with which that big salmon had leisurely explored the waters of his small home.

There were still federal CETA (Comprehensive Employment Training Act) funds available in the late seventies, left over from Lyndon Johnson's strategy for a Great Society. Richard got his hands on some of these funds and pioneered a style of backwoods stream rehabilitation. It was a three-mile hike in wild country to a series of logjams on Indian Creek in the Eel River basin, where the jams had diverted the stream's flow against an unstable bank, dumping sediment onto some of the best spawning gravels in the drainage. Richard put together a small crew of irregulars, along with whatever tools could be scrounged and were lightweight enough to be packed in over several miles of rough terrain. A retired horse that had been left in Richard's safekeeping was pressed into service. The horse not only served as a pack animal but also provided the energy that powered a crude windlass used to haul single logs out of the jams. The logs themselves were then used to build and anchor a cribwall to protect the eroding banks against the force of the stream. Large rocks and logs were moved to create step pools that salmon and steelhead would be able to use to make their way through the modified jams to more spawning areas upstream.

After two summers of work, the results were beautiful—and effective. Richard and his crew were not practicing primitive engineering so much as evolving an art form that used wood and water and soil as its media. When Richard and his son Maseo hiked out to the project site in the November following the last summer of work, the area stank with rotting salmon carcasses. The end of the project had happily coincided with a great year in the ocean salmon population; when the anomalously large numbers of salmon had beaten their way up Indian Creek that year, they had found the large stretch of reclaimed spawning habitat that was the end product of a new sort of collaboration between species. Now Richard was on fire: perhaps he had stumbled on a pathway toward making it right.

This morning I don't need to explain the pressures of the moment to Richard; he knows them as well as I do.

"I've got to meet a guy in Ettersburg who's got a starter motor," he says. "Let's get the fish safe, and then I'll come back and help you. I have a meeting at eight, but that should give us plenty of time to get the weir out of the water."

Up on the flat above the river, we've installed and plumbed a long fiberglass watering trough and attached a hinged wooden lid to it. The trough will easily hold four to six captured fish, along with their tubes. Enough filtered spring water runs through it to keep the salmon alive for the few days it might take before the females' eggs are ready for fertilization. We use it only in situations like this because previous experience has taught us that the eggs ripen more slowly if the salmon are removed from the river; we don't know why. But if we don't move our new guests now, we are in danger of losing them.

Richard climbs into one of the extra sets of chestwaders hanging in the jumble of damp gear in the back of the trailer. We are in luck and find a size ten that fits him perfectly. Three salmon tubes are still tethered along the shallows of the river—the large female I found last night and the two smaller males captured earlier. The larger tube takes two of us to handle it, one at either end. As we lift the tube out of the water, the salmon panics and begins to beat her tail frantically against its walls. The sound fills both Richard and me with adrenaline. We have performed this routine before, and we don't need to speak. Our feet, made clumsy by the heavy waders, find footholds on the steep bank, the tube between us held level so as not to injure the fish. Without thinking, we work together like a single organism, two men and a fish; we *run* up the embankment without stumbling. With his free hand, Richard raises the cover of the trough and we ease the fish in her tube into the container, her head facing the intake. She quiets down in the dark and steady flow.

The remaining tubes are small enough for each of us to take one, and we make the run again, Richard and I, each holding a heavy tube in front of us. Now I am breathing hard and feeling the effects of interrupted sleep the night before. The rain has picked up. With a little wind behind them, the big drops are stinging my face. The steep banks of the gorge are liquid sheets and rivulets of runoff. The water from the air has found a channel in the crease of my hood: the collar of my shirt beneath is soaked. A low branch catches me in the face and I go down at the top of the gorge, hard enough to knock the wind out of me. The tube is vibrating with the struggle of the fish inside. I haven't lost my grip on it, but now it is above my head like a set of weights. Before I can catch my breath and understand how to right myself, Richard has returned. He takes the tube from my hands as if he were catching a baby falling through the air and finishes the run to the trough.

Richard is still grinning his crazy grin as he pulls away.

"Back in a flash, man."

I sit down to catch my breath and measure the odds of his parting remark being accurate. I know how these things go. Ettersburg is forty-five minutes away on twisting mountain roads. Maybe Richard will find his man with the starter motor where the man said he would be; maybe he won't. Rarely do the three bolts that hold the starter to a rusty old Chevy engine come out without stripping the threads on at least one of them, and the starter won't function without all three bolts firmly in place. It might take all afternoon searching through various spare parts stashes to find a bolt that will fit. Then there will be the question of whether or not any of the wrenches on hand will fit the head of the new bolt. The starter motor itself, salvaged from an engine that had been sitting idle for years, might or might not crank over.

I would love to sit and wait for Richard to return, maybe take a nap, but the river has risen another inch or two in the last half hour. After catching my breath, I duck inside the trailer, remove the heavy Helly-Hansen raincoat and dry my hands on the all-purpose towel hanging on the door. Hands dry enough to light a cigarette, I weigh my options. Who knows when Richard will return?

I'm going to need to find Stevie.

I have noticed that all men have a liking for some special animal, tree, plant, or spot of earth. If men would pay more attention to these preferences and seek what is best to do to make themselves worthy of that toward which they are so attracted, they might have dreams which would purify their lives.

ATTRIBUTED TO BRAVE BUFFALO, A SIOUX ELDER

STEVIE'S PORTABLE HOME of the season is an old camper shell set down on a couple of pieces of plywood. Like a snail, he has moved his shell to the trap site for the duration of the winter trapping season. A slab of foam affords him a bed; two plastic milk crates constitute his cabinetry. Stevie borrowed ten dollars yesterday, ten dollars I knew would be invested in jug wine to be used as entry to whatever celebration he could find on New Year's Eve—ten dollars I know I will never see again. It hadn't surprised me when I peeked inside his shelter this morning and found him gone. Stevie would have sampled whatever celebratory substances were available the night before, and would have kept on sampling for as long as he could stand up.

By now it is well into afternoon—the iron-gray light filtered through rain and forest canopy offers little clue as to how much time remains before total darkness descends. When I check the camper shell again, Stevie is there, curled in his dirty sleeping bag. I shake his foot. With a sweetness of temperament that never fails to startle me, he opens his one good eye, smiles, and says, "Well, hullo Freeman." Sitting up, he searches with one hand for his baseball cap while the other roots hopefully for an unopened can of Coors. Finding one, he grins again, pops it open and takes a long pull.

Now I tell him about last night's catch. He scrambles out of his bag fully dressed, pulls on his barn boots, and lopes down to the river to take a look, ignoring the rain. When he returns the can of Coors is empty and Stevie is full of energy, ready to muscle his way through any job the world might throw at him.

Stevie takes a large part of his identity from the few years he has spent fishing for salmon commercially, crewing on the little day boats of the Mosquito Fleet out of nearby Shelter Cove as long as there were fish to support it. Then he worked for a couple of years on Peter Van Arsdale's boat, which was large enough to pursue the tuna that run two hundred miles off the coast. It is as a fisherman that he returns from checking out our situation.

Stevie has understood the job before us without a word being exchanged. "River's rising," he says as he pulls off his boots and struggles into his waders.

In the world of natural provision, anadromous fish—fish that leave the oceans and ascend freshwater rivers and streams to breed—present a special case. Salmon take their growth from the nutrients of the sea in places where they themselves are less available to human predation. Then, when they have reached the peak of flavor and nutritional value, they deliver themselves as food for all the carnivores and omnivores that live on the rivers and streams that flow to the sea. Most other species are happy to wait until the reproductive process is finished before the flesh of the fish is eaten, and most salmon is consumed as carrion. Bears and eagles occasionally take a gravid salmon, but this would be an exception. Among the myriad eaters of these fish, only otters, seals and sea lions, and humans take salmon as they cross over from salt water to fresh—before they have reproduced.

Humans, however, unlike the other predators at the mouths of rivers, build effective technologies for the capture of more fish than can be eaten immediately, and other technologies for the preservation and storage of food for long periods of time. These technologies, even at their most primitive, give humans the power to do serious harm to the security of their own natural provision. Among the simplest technologies is one that has the greatest potential to harm the run: the fish dam across the river. These simple structures, whether built of brush or rock, or more elaborately of wood and wire, block the river to upstream migration and have the capacity to destroy a whole race of salmon in a period of a few years, unless they are used with great care.

There is a painting made by George Catlin in 1833 that depicts the snowshoe dance of the Ojibwa or Chippewa people of Northeastern North America.[1] It is a picture truly worth a bookful of words on the working relationship between a community and its tools. A dozen men are dancing with snowshoes on their feet, each carrying a spear or bow; they circle on a fresh layer of snow. Two dancers carry intricately carved rattles to provide rhythm while a third carries a pair of snowshoes elevated at the end of a pole. The mood of the painting is muscular, active, joyous—it moves. The dancers are ritually recognizing the advantage the snowshoe gives them over their snowbound winter prey. Repeating

such a ritual annually at first snowfall reinforces a respect for
the power of the tool and makes it less likely that the hunter
will take his advantage for granted and grow profligate in
his killing.

Aboriginal peoples on the Pacific Rim were quick to
understand the powers of their technologies, and the dangers that their traps and weirs and nets posed to salmon.
They understood the double-edged power of tools, which
give humans an ecological advantage as well as the power to
destroy their provision. One way that indigenous peoples
dealt with the paradox of their tool-making skills was to sa-
cralize and ritualize the technologies themselves.

In all of northwestern California, the largest and most
elaborate social event of the year before 1848 is said to have
been the building of the fish dam at Kepel, near the confluence of the Trinity and Klamath Rivers. This highly formalized event occupied a hundred or more men and their
families for ten days, exactly, and thousands of ritualized
person-hours went into the construction of the weir across
the river each year. Once completed, the structure was
fished for just ten more days, regardless of the size of the run
or the number of fish caught, and then it was opened up and
abandoned, to be built anew the next year.

Each step of the process—the cutting of the poles, their
placement in the river, the ceremonies required before fishing began—was informed by such complex ritual content
that the role of remembering the exact procedures and su-
pervising the event each year was invested in one man, called
a formulist by the anthropologists. This role was his for life,
and it was his responsibility to select and train his assistants,
as well as his replacement for the next generation. It required
his total attention for as much as four months of each year.

After the structures were abandoned at the end of ten August days, he and his assistants remained in a hut above the dam site to be sure that it was washed away by early winter storms, so as not to interfere with later runs of other stocks of salmon.[2]

The last fish dam at Kepel was built in 1906. In 1916, Lucy Thompson (Che-na-wah Weitch-ah-wah), a Yurok born in 1853, put down her memories of a nearly vanished culture:

In these traps, there get to be a mass of salmon, so full they make the whole structure of the fish dam quiver and tremble with their weight, by holding the water from passing through the lattice-work freely. After all have taken what they want of the salmon, which must be done in the early part of the day, Lock [the dam formulist] or Lock-nee [a younger male assistant] opens the upper gates of the traps and lets the salmon pass on up the river, and at the same time great numbers are passing through the open gap at the south side of the river. This is done so the Hoopas on up the Trinity River have a chance at the salmon catching. But they keep a close watch to see that there are enough left to effect the spawning, by which the supply is kept up for the following year.[3]

Old photos of similar dams built by tribes upstream reveal the same openings so that fish might pass through. Such practices guaranteed the reproduction of the salmon along the length of the river and its tributaries, and insured that the people who lived upstream would also have a share of the flesh to eat. The elaborate and lengthy annual ritual must also have had the effect of animating the technology itself, of investing it with a sacred and relational life of its own: the tool is brought into the community as a working member; to treat it as inanimate, to use it sloppily or greedily, would have been equivalent to treating a member of one's family in a similar way.

This single communal practice, however, would not by itself have assured the continuity of salmon runs over the centuries. Yurok territory stretches from the estuary of the Klamath River upstream some sixty miles to its confluence with a large tributary, the Trinity. Further upstream and along the Trinity River, live the Hupa. Further upstream yet and along another large tributary, the Salmon River, the Karuk live. While the Kepel dam may have been the largest event in the salmon year, it was only one event embedded in an annual cycle of ritual self-regulation that was shared by the several tribes and determined the timing and distribution of fishing practices.

The most significant rites of regulation were performed at the beginning of the spring run of kings on the Klamath, when the first fresh salmon of the year enter the river. This was the leanest time of the food-year—a time when the stored acorns were beginning to mold, when last year's dried salmon were beginning to grow stringy and tasteless, before spring greens had grown large enough to eat. How mouths must have watered and stomachs growled in anticipation of the first rich taste of fresh salmon. Yet from one end of the vast river system to another, people were restrained from casual consumption of the fish until certain ceremonial practices were performed at specific locations.

The specifics of the "first salmon" ceremonies varied from place to place and people to people, but they had several characteristics in common. They induced restraint through the means of powerful taboos: "Fresh salmon could not be consumed by any member of the community until the first spring salmon ritual took place. Supernaturally induced illness or death would occur if the taboo surrounding the capture of salmon were broken."[4] Consumption of fresh fish was delayed until the first fish had been prepared and eaten ceremonially, after which a communal feast often took place, with assurances that all get fed. By now each delectable morsel of roasted salmon contains more than meat for the

protein-starved: it contains the message of the full importance of the relationship between humans and their sources
of provision.

These ceremonial practices also had the general effect of
delaying generalized fishing until a small but significant portion of the early run had passed through to spawn. Anthropologists Sean Swezey and Robert Heizer speculate that

in allowing the salmon to run freely during the initial period of ritual restriction (the duration and timing of which was controlled
by the formulist, and generally appears to have lasted from several
days to two weeks), riverine tribes maintained a productive inventory of *spawning* salmon each spring, which ensured successful
reproduction of the king salmon runs in following years. Intensive
salmon fishing *after* the period of ritual restriction, by large numbers of individuals initiating this subsistence effort at the same
time, probably benefitted the production of salmon by preventing
over-crowding at the spawning beds. . . . The maintenance and
conservation of the salmon subsistence on a year-to-year basis was
perhaps the most important function of the first-salmon observance, and there is no evidence that native populations ever seriously overfished.[5]

After the initial first salmon ceremony was performed at
the Yurok village of Welkwau, near the mouth of the river,
strong young runners took the message upstream to the
Hupa people. There, near the present town of Hoopa, ten
days of ceremony and prayer were conducted before the
people were allowed to fish. The Karuk conducted their first
salmon observances at Amaikiaram, near present-day Somes
Bar. Here the community at large, perhaps hungrier because
they had waited longer, removed themselves to the hills surrounding while the sacred first fish was taken and ritually
eaten by spiritual leaders. When the people returned to the
village, fishing and feasting began.

Widely accepted modern models of human nature as
driven by greed and self-interest (as exemplified by Garrett

Hardin's arguments in his often-quoted *Tragedy of the Commons*) would lead us to expect one people warring against another over the salmon runs of the Klamath basin until one group dominates the resource, or the resource is destroyed. The earliest anthropologists, however, discovered an entirely different picture. They found a largely trilingual people with elaborate trail systems between their homelands. These trails were used by young runners to keep the peoples abreast of the movement of salmon and relay the news that appropriate rituals had been performed that signalled that now fish could be taken. Fishing rights combined the intimate management of individual reaches and eddies of the river, by families who maintained exclusive use of such sites, with a communal use of larger dams like Kepel. Collective cultural practices were built around the life of the river rather than on conflict between user groups, and this was accomplished without sacrificing the diversity of unique tribal identities. The anthropologists found a shared tradition of intertribal ritual self-regulation that seems to have risen right out of the river.

That these cultural conservation strategies were successful and enduring cannot be denied. Conflicting estimates of annual consumption of salmon by tribes in the Klamath-Trinity basin range between half a million and two million pounds. There may have been that much variation in seasonal abundance anyway. Indigenous peoples could have taken more, but they didn't. Fishermen in the cannery-driven fishery that replaced the native one could take more, and did. The industrial fishery peaked out with a catch of 1.4 million pounds in 1912, and has been in steady decline ever since.

We know many of these details through the writings of white observers between 1851, when gold seekers began to pour into the area, and the first two decades of the twentieth century, when Alfred Kroeber and his students were conducting their first systematic surveys of indigenous life even as it was in an advanced stage of disintegration. What they were seeing had to be the culmination of centuries-long struggles between peoples of significantly diverse cultures to bring themselves to a point of peaceful coexistence within the constraints and opportunities presented by the life of the river basin that was their common home. Only Lucy Thompson gives us a glimpse into the difficulties of that struggle toward a system of social mutualism that resulted in the peoples of the Klamath basin developing an enduring reciprocal relationship between humans and their common watershed.

The Klamath [Yurok] Indians as a tribe are like other people that have a history dating back long before the great flood, as their legends plainly tell. They have had their wars and plenty of them, through all the ages, and never laid down their bows and spears at any time to any other tribe or tribes, and have at different times had to fight every tribe, and sometimes combinations of tribes. They have many times been nearly exterminated at different places of inhabitation.[6]

Each tribal grouping in the lower Klamath basin speaks a different language, and these languages are derived from entirely different linguistic families, indicating that the tribes immigrated into the area from different points of origin and probably arrived at different times over the centuries. The Yurok language is of the Algonquian stock, related to those spoken on the East Coast and in the heartland of North America. Hupas speak a variation of the Athabaskan family, other variations of which are spoken all the way from the Alaskan interior to the territory of the Navajo. The Karuk language is of the Hokan stock, perhaps the most ancient of the protolanguages.

I don't know who arrived when, nor have I run across anyone who does. It is no longer important. Each tribe has legends that take its local inhabitation back into an antiquity beyond memory. But each new immigration must have created upheavals as profound as those by which twentieth-century people are benumbed. The system of river and ridgeline pathways that were the communication corridors of coordinated self-regulation by the time of contact must have grown by trial and error over hundreds of years. The long process that led finally to an enduring balance must have included wars and feuds, intolerance and enslavement, starvation and displacement. Some people left to seek less heavily inhabited places. (I have a pet theory that this may account for the origins of the aboriginal Mattole people. The Mattole spoke an Athabaskan language similar to Hupa. Paleolinguists trace the differentiation of the two languages to a period roughly a thousand years ago.) Yet over and over again, salmon kept drawing people back from the cusp of failure to try again to establish peaceful coexistence in and with their beautiful valleys.

Or so I like to imagine. It is important to me. I am drawn back to this sort of dreaming whenever I reach a point of despair about our difficulties in communicating with our neighbors about land management practices. I don't believe we have a thousand years. Neither do we have any choice but to take the time it takes to do things right. The Salmon Group had already had a taste of the larger forces arrayed against it: the destructive effects of recent resource extraction, the interpenetration of big government and big money, the entropy of large institutions. But as of 1983 we'd had little experience of how demanding and difficult it would be to reach consensus about a common future within our own watershed. Even though we speak the same language. Even though our cultural differences seem small compared to the ones I've been discussing. (By the time I am writing, in 1998, I will have experienced carefully nurtured new friendships dissolved in the firefight of political disputes. I will have seen families fall apart, in part because of the demands of the work. I will have seen promising alliances grow to a place of great promise and then collapse out of their inability to grow further. Some people will have left to seek less, or more, intensely inhabited places.)

I try to imagine what quality of mind maintained that determination over centuries to sink deep into the landscape, what learning processes occurred along the way that finally led to the elegant balance between people and place. My modern mind wants a formula for progress, step-by step instructions, codified methodologies. But when I look to the history of the Klamath peoples for clues, it always comes back to the same things. *Pay attention to the landscape. Pay attention to what the animals are saying to you. Look to the long term.*

In a document written recently by a work team from the Karuk tribe for the Klamath National Forest as part of a watershed analysis for the Salmon River, I come across these lines:

> Close, lifelong observation of nature and the landscape is much admired in the Karuk culture. . . . Indian children have early on been placed in a life trajectory which establishes, at the deepest levels of the mind, habits of quiet observation and a sense that they are not necessarily in control of the world around them. . . . When people's actions are influenced by keen observation of nature, they are much less likely to attempt to dominate or desire to change natural processes.[7]

A man named Frank Lake hears of my interest through mutual friends and comes by to visit. Frank was born to his passion for studying traditional lifeways. His step-mother is Yurok and his father, of Karuk descent, is Bobbie Lake-Thom, professor of native studies for twenty years at the California State University. As a trained biologist, Frank is fascinated by the ecological implications of aboriginal practices. He hopes to find a path forward for contemporary people by analyzing the long-term effects of the cultivation of the wild practiced by his ancestors.

Frank brings with him a sampling of some of the traditional ceremonial regalia he painstakingly creates in his spare time—necklaces of shells and pine nuts, soapstone pipes. He is proud that some of his regalia is so well done that it is used in the dances that are being revived in Klamath territory.

After his long drive from the inland National Forest in Oregon where he works, Frank is delighted when I suggest a walk on the ocean beach. He gathers shells as we walk. Each shell has a story and a technique for converting it to revelatory costume. The shells rattle in his pouch, and as he talks I imagine them clicking and rustling rhythmically in the skirts of dancers. In the evening he walks me through the literature on Kepel, cross-referencing as he goes to the geography of the Klamath River. It's important to him to know just *where* this or that happened—more important than when, or in what sequence. He likes to go out and sit in those specific places, see what additional information the place can provide. It's another thing he does in his spare time.

I ask him how he thinks that quality of attentiveness works in cultural evolution. When he answers, his scientific training falls away and his ancestral heritage takes over.

"The way I was brought up is that if you went out to a place, and you prayed and you stayed clean, and you were strict on yourself, you were shown certain things. So that life itself is trial and error, but often there were jumps in evolutionary development that became a spiritual knowledge. Those are the ways that big evolutionary jumps happen. Those are the big turning points."

🐟 Thirty years before, eavesdropping on an interview of ecologist Sterling Bunnel by Peter Berg, I had heard Bunnel make speculations that played a large part in my own life trajectory.

Most of the day tends to come through in terms of a kind of spontaneous mental image. So that if you're living in an area with a certain type of landscape and a certain kind of patterning, your mind is going to run to certain kinds of patterns . . . almost programmed by the kind of input you're getting. Actually you find that there's a tremendous correspondence between different kinds of plant and animal life with different types of geological formation, something you can see down at the mountain. Look up on the mountain and different strata of rock are diagrammed by different types of bushes growing. You can see it.[8]

And I *could* see it. If those patterns on the mountainside had a part in forming the very structure of my mind, then the same patterns must contain a language I might yet learn.

🐟 The industrial-age people who came later built fish wheels just inside the mouth of many salmon rivers—including the Klamath. A weir guided the fish to the large water wheel; buckets mounted on the wheel delivered them to bins on barges. Downstream of the wheels on larger rivers like the Columbia, horse-drawn seines competed with small boats trailing long gill nets. Fishing technologies evolved and proliferated as extensions of the individual or user-group imagination.

It took a while for salmon populations to be understood as

a public benefit and therefore an object of government regulation. This insight usually coincided with an alarming diminishment in salmon production and was inevitably followed by a generation or more of debate swirling around the rights of individuals and what powers were invested in government. Governments, when they did finally act, often found that the only way to govern equitably in regard to the many individuals and entities that benefit from the fishery was to create laws which modified or banned outright whole technologies. Gill net mesh sizes were regulated; open and closed seasons established; the percentage of river width that any weir could block was gradually diminished. Finally, after twenty-five, forty, and nearly fifty years of decline of salmon populations, fish wheels were outlawed in California, Oregon, and Washington respectively. In all except the largest rivers, commercial fishers were eventually banished to the sea to chase fish in diesel-gobbling boats—chasing fish that were trying hard to deliver themselves to human settlement.

This process has had the perverse effect over time of restricting fishing methods to those that are *least* effective, a progression that has in turn produced a few interesting side effects. In California, for instance, the commercial salmon fishery was finally restricted to a hook-and-line technology called trolling. Trolling boats could put out no more than six lines, each with three baited hooks. It doesn't take a very large boat to mount such gear; trollers tend to organize themselves into one- and two-person operations; and a single person could get started with a small open boat and a couple of hand lines. On some level, ritual and regulation had come full circle to meet each other in the middle. Men and women working singly or in pairs were once more forced into an intimate relation with their prey. And, in that the experience of fishing from a small boat radically alters perceptual experience and creates a set of nonnegotiable relationships with the moods of the sea, it could be said that fishing technology had once again become sacralized. On a small boat, the technology remains a part of the worker's value system, rather than the worker being subsumed by the machine, as on a factory ship. But fishermen, along with the rest of us, have lost the knowledge of the place-specific nature of our nurturance. We were chasing our food over the vast open pastures of the great sea. We lost our sense of place and community, and then we lost our fisheries.

As I write, these small, localized California fisheries—some of our last ambassadors to the wild—have also been driven off the water by a century of institutional mismanagement organized to meet the demands of a globalized economy.

Stevie is not fishing in 1983; so few salmon are being caught at sea as to make the Mosquito Fleet unprofitable even for those with little capital invested. But during his fishing years, Stevie seemed to have found in salmon a thread of continuity with the wild world along which he could make some sense of an otherwise chaotic life. I never see Stevie except during the period from Thanksgiving to a few weeks into January, when the salmon are running. The fish trap is near the headwaters of the river, and my home is far downstream, near the mouth. I know little of what Stevie does during the rest of the year; I don't really want to know.

The wide spot in the river where the fish trap is located used to be called the Stanley Hole because it was formed at the place where little Stanley Creek pours into the main stream of the river. It was once a popular swimming spot. Now it is shallowed up by sediments washed downstream from the heavy logging of fifteen years earlier. It is easy to see the aggradation of the river as an analog to the disintegration of the local community: the spot is now known as the Dump Hole. There is a pull-out on the county road here that's littered with black plastic bags full of household trash. Junkies who don't want to take their habit home—or who have no home—use this spot, hidden from the road itself by a scrim of second-growth redwoods, as an open-air shooting gallery whenever the weather is pleasant. Between the black plastic bags it's not hard to find discarded hypodermics and homemade "outfits."

But when David and Gary and I, the downstream members of the Salmon Group, arrive early each winter to set up the trap, the place is clean. Our cohort will have known exactly when the berm at the mouth of the river has broken and the gravid fish have entered. In the two or three weeks it takes for the fish to beat their way upstream, while we work furiously to get our gear together, Stevie—who knows the fish are on the way by some means that still remains a mystery—will be hauling trash to the local landfill in a borrowed truck, scouring the grounds of drug paraphernalia and condoms and bottles. By the time we arrive with our truckloads of weir panels and trap parts, holding tubes and winches and cables, our trailer and tents, Stevie will have the place looking like a genteel community campground with a year-round maintenance crew. He will also have been wandering the upstream reaches of the river, alert to the arrival of the first fish and prepared to discourage the remnant poachers who don't know they might be taking out the last hope of one of the last native king salmon runs in California. One hears stories of Stevie, a tight bundle of fury, facing down men larger than himself who are armed with sharp gaff hooks.

It might be accurate to say that Stevie uses the salmon season to clean himself up, to bring his toxic activities down to a more sustainable, less life-threatening level. But it is more completely correct, I think, to say that his experience of the lives of salmon has created a context in which he can act out even larger survival instincts. During those years spent fishing, Stevie learned something from salmon that made sense in a way that nothing else had made sense before. He had experienced on the fishing boats a context for living clean and sober that was deeply, essentially right.

Each fish brought up from the deep carries with it implications of the Other, the great life of the sea that lies permanently beyond anyone's feeble strivings to control or understand it. This is information received and stored in the body; it may or may not be available for mental deconstruction and articulation; it is reinforced by the memory of the muscles and nerves, which when one is on a boat are constantly working to maintain balance in response to the long, rolling swells of the ocean. True immersion in a system larger than oneself carries with it exposure to a vast complexity wherein joy and terror are complementary parts. Life and death are no longer opposite poles of individual existence but parts of a pattern so large that the only adequate response is surrender.

It's raining hard now, and a south wind is up. As the sun retreats west somewhere beyond the iron-gray ceiling that obscures it, the light is dimmed further by the water blown through the air. The tops of my waders reach only as far as my solar plexus. When Stevie and I walk into the river, water as brown as Mexican chocolate swirls around us, waist-high, running with enough power so that one false step could tumble either of us in. The weir panels are trying to tear themselves loose from the posts that hold them up, from the sandbags that hold them down. The metal fence posts are beginning to assume a precarious tilt downstream.

It seems a different place than the one in which I worked

last night. The placid back eddy has disappeared under three feet of racing water. My attention is divided: with my eyes I try to keep myself headed in a straight line while at the same time scanning the flow upstream for any debris the river might be carrying toward us; my feet are feeling cautiously for the cobbles or holes that might throw me off balance and into the flow. (A favorite story told in many variations around campfires at night concerns the fisherman who takes a fall and is pulled under by the weight of the water that fills his waders.)

The first thing to do is recover the sandbags that hold the wire apron at the bottom of the weir panels tight against the bottom of the channel, recycled plastic feed sacks filled with forty dry pounds of gravel and sand. The top edges of the feed sacks have unraveled and the individual strands of plastic wave in the current like dead white hair, barely perceptible through the muddy water. Hook one with a gaff on the end of a four-foot handle, haul it to the surface, grab it with the left hand and hook another: carry out two at a time to maintain balance. Do it again. Pile them far enough up the bank so that rising water won't take them back. There are some sixty sandbags.

Stevie keeps up a constant chatter punctuated with exclamations, curses, and comments on the color of the water, the debris it carries, the heaviness of the waterlogged bags. He laments the fact that we are not capturing the fish that are probably swimming past our legs right now. His running commentary irritates me—I'm feeling the lack of sleep from the night before—and I can barely make out the content of what he's saying above the roar of the water. But I pay attention to where his voice is coming from; we want to stay close should one or the other of us go down. We are both remembering the tedium of filling the bags and wiring them shut, and we want to save them to use another day. We also want to leave the river tidy. But by the time we've made ten trips each, the light has dimmed perceptibly and our legs are getting weak. We pull the rest of the bags a foot or two upstream and leave them on the bottom of the channel, hoping that their weight will hold them there until the water recedes.

The weir panels are secured to the fence posts by short lengths of parachute cord tied in a slip knot, one above the level of the flow and another under the water just at the end of arm's reach. If the knots are tangled, a knife to cut the line. I've lost seventy dollars' worth of Swiss Army knives over the past two years, good knives that slipped from my hand while I was groping blindly under water. I wonder where they have got to by now, how far down stream, and whether they are buried in gravel and mud or if their bright red handles flash in some riffle still, occasionally mistaken for food by a passing steelhead.

Once free, the panels slam against our chests and we wrestle them out of the water to carry them to shore held over our heads. Fourteen of them. They are light but we move more slowly now, made more vulnerable because we are no longer able to use our arms for balance. I think of high-wire artists and the long poles they carry to make minute adjustments to their poise. I think of them as dilettantes. I think about anything at all except the burning fatigue in my legs and now in my arms and back.

The wind is blowing harder, driving the rain in lateral sheets that sting my face and cause me to squint, cause me to forget to keep a part of my attention on the flow upstream. Stevie's running monologue, which by this time has become one more element of background noise along with the pounding of the water and the rush of the wind through the

trees, rises to a shout. "Watch out!" and I take a little leap to
avoid being struck by a broken branch coming at me at thirty
miles an hour. The leap carries me no more than a foot,
enough to avoid the branch, but one foot comes down on a
slippery round boulder and I come near to going over. The
little surge of adrenaline is welcome. We climb out of the
river and sit on the bank to rest. We try to smoke cigarettes,
but the frail tubes of tobacco are soaked before we can get
them lit. The two panels nearest the far shore remain to be
carried out, but darkness is approaching quickly; we can
barely make them out thirty feet away through the gloom.
We get our headlamps from the trailer and finish the job in
the dark. Once the panels are out, we work the metal fence
posts back and forth, back and forth, all the time exerting
whatever upward pressure we can until the posts come loose
and can be heaved up onto the nearest bank.

And then we are done. The trailer smells now of our wet
clothes hung around the open mouth of the little oven to dry.
A pot of tea, more cheese and crackers. The discovery of a
ripe avocado in the ice chest restores us, as does the two
inches of port wine left in the bottom of a bottle.

We talk about the work. I am tired and gloomy, focused
on the half of the glass that is empty. Are our feeble efforts
really increasing the success rate of the spawning king
salmon? I tell Stevie about the spawning pair I saw earlier today, downstream. Even if the high water we just climbed out
of doesn't bury the redd in cobble, silt may settle out into the
pockets of air around the eggs and smother most of them as
the water draws down. I'd be surprised if 10 percent of the
fertilized eggs survive. Only two hundred fry, say, might
emerge from the nest, I complain. Of those, half will be
eaten by mergansers or year-old steelhead or river otters before they get to the estuary. Some of them will get trapped

in the summer lagoon and high temperatures will kill most
of these. Of those that cross into salt water, another half will
die before reaching the feeding grounds of the deeper ocean.
It'll be a miracle if even one adult survives the tiny fishing
fleet to return to the mouth of the river.

I am thinking of the Salmon Group's agreement with the
state Department of Fish and Game, which allows us to take
eighty thousand eggs for incubation. We aren't even close
and the season is drawing to an end. The DFG has granted us
all of two thousand dollars this year to accomplish our goal.
We have spent as much time raising money as we have on the
fish trap, and that time will be doubled again by the volunteers who will keep the little backyard hatcheries operating
in the months to come. There are too few of us, a couple of
dozen harried idealists working against what seem to be all
the forces of nature and human stupidity.

Stevie keeps trying to interrupt my flood of complaints,
but I override him, all the poisonous accumulations of three
days of interrupted sleep transformed into easy anger. When
I am finally finished, Stevie gives me a patient lesson in op-
timism.

Stevie is a guy who sees the glass as half full. Even with
a hangover and little sleep, he bubbles with enthusiasm. He
reminds me of the eggs we have already taken and fertilized,
safe in an incubator up the hill. If our luck holds as it has for
the last two years, better than 80 percent of the eggs will
turn into young king salmon. The female captured last night
will add another four thousand or so eggs to our numbers.

"What if you were panning for gold, Freeman? Wouldn't
you be glad for every fleck you saw in the bottom of your pan?
Think of the eggs that way! Put 'em in your little bag and stuff
'em under your pillow and have sweet dreams about the big
party they'll buy you." The eggs that hatch out will be kept

safe in rearing ponds covered with bird-netting for two whole months before they are released back into the wild, Stevie reminds me. When they cross the continental shelf, they'll be fatter, faster than their fellows. "They'll *outrun* all those predators lurking out there. Or at least some of them will. Those eggs are going to produce dozens of new spawners, man, dozens! You'll eat their offspring when you're old."

I feel old right now. Some of my self-pity has evaporated as I listen to Stevie, but I can't help comparing his numbers to the estimate made by the Fish and Wildlife Service nearly twenty years ago, that a functional Mattole River could accommodate up to eighteen thousand spawning salmon. We know that less than a thousand fish are using the river by now, in the winter of 1982–83, maybe many fewer—maybe only dozens! How many years will it take of our bleary-eyed, seat-of-the-pants efforts to bring those numbers back up?

Our banter winds down into punch-drunk arithmetic. By the time our adrenaline wears away, the numbers hang empty of meaning in the dank air of the trailer. We have just enough energy to check the flow of water in the holding tanks and the pretty little incubator box before we stumble back into our beds.

If the rain continues, the river will remain too high to reinstall the weir. I will drive my truck home tomorrow, sleep in my own bed with Nina. I hope the rain goes on for days. An hour ago I'd been ready to quit, but as I drift off into a sleep full of watery dreams, I know that I'll be back.

In science, a house vacant of facts is usually haunted by theories.

RICHARD NELSON, *Heart and Blood*

$\mathcal{E}$VEN AS THE self-regulatory behaviors of aboriginal peoples in the range of the Pacific salmon were being lost, new belief systems having to do with a human relationship to natural provision were taking hold.

The earliest American fish hatcheries were dedicated to the idea, imported from Europe, that productive fish stocks could be introduced from one place to another for the benefit of human consumption. It was an idea enthusiastically embraced by the lay practitioners of "progressive" nineteenth-century science, usually entrepreneurs with both feet planted firmly on the ground of commercial benefit. Hatcheries were an attempt, in many cases wildly successful, to apply the methods of industry and agriculture to wild fish, and as such they fit perfectly into the national strategy for the conquest and development of the American West.

The rage for artificial propagation of fishes began in New York and New Hampshire, partially in response to the near-total diminishment of river-run fishes in Eastern streams.[1]

The output of the local propagation efforts quickly exceeded the market demand for their products and led to the formation of the American Fish Culturists' Association, whose stated purpose was "to keep ahead of man's harmful actions on rivers, streams, and lakes to the detriment of fish and fishing." Hidden in the Association's idealistic statement was the commercial ambition to expand its activities into the cornucopia of development opportunities in the American West. Within a year of its formation, the organization had successfully lobbied the newly formed United States Fish Commission (USFC) to send the Association's secretary, Livingston Stone, to California, to establish a salmon hatchery on the McCloud River. "We have tilled the ground four thousand years," wrote Seth Green, an associate of Stone's, "we have just begun to till the water."[2]

The USFC was headed by Spencer Baird, assistant secretary to the Smithsonian Institution and a highly respected naturalist. Baird was convinced that "policy and education [could] triumph over every disadvantage [to keep pace] with the inevitable exhaustion of the native fish life . . . [accompanying] the development of the country and the increase of population." This conviction was perfectly in keeping with the laissez-faire government policies of the time regarding natural resources. Historian Arthur McEvoy notes that the underlying premise of the USFC was that

the degradation of previously "unexploited" resources under the impact of commercial civilization was no less inevitable than the disappearance of Indians and buffalo from the continent. . . . Laissez-faire ideology held that attempts to bring such social forces under control through the deliberate use of law were by nature vicious . . . [or,] if they did not go that far, Baird and his comrades considered them pointless in any event.[3]

While Baird and the Commission would go on to initiate the earliest and some of the most extensive inventories of fisheries conditions in America, his most popular program by far was the introduction of nonnative food fishes into depleted rivers during the last few decades of the nineteenth century. This was the driving force behind the development of the hatchery movement: not the augmentation of wild stocks so much as the application of models of industrial agriculture to fisheries. Over the next century, hatcheries would bring about disturbances to aquatic ecosystems so far-reaching that we are still sorting them out, all the while employing technology that has never, until very recently, been any more than peripherally informed by the requirements of wild populations.

As McEvoy puts it, "Although Baird and others paid homage to the need to control harvesting and environmental degradation, promising to sustain the economy's supply of fish without interrupting existing patterns of use yielded far greater political rewards."[4] When the USFC allocated five thousand dollars for the construction of a salmon hatchery in California in 1872, it was not for the purpose of protecting or preserving California's already diminishing salmon runs, but rather to ship fertilized Pacific salmon eggs to the East Coast for introduction into depleted rivers that drained into the Atlantic.

A Unitarian minister, Livingston Stone (1836–1912) abandoned his ministry at a relatively young age to pursue the vision that would occupy him for the rest of his life. He understood himself as a conservationist in a time when for most people *conserve* was a word relating mostly to root cellars and home-canned fruit. His efforts were driven by a peculiarly nineteenth-century combination of idealism and entrepreneurial energies. His unacknowledged ignorance of the systems with which he was tampering was matched only by his faith in the ability of humans to organize them for their own benefit. He pursued his avocation vigorously and on a large scale, and unwittingly managed to commit serious ecological damages in a time before the word *ecology* had even been coined.[5]

Stone was thirty-six when he reached the McCloud, a headwaters tributary of the Sacramento, with two younger assistants, one of them his nephew. To a country full of rough veterans of the gold rush he brought an anomalous gentility in the form of his Harvard education and Unitarian tolerance. He also brought tremendous energy and zeal.

He and his two helpers first spent some weeks surveying the length of the Sacramento River from its confluence with the San Francisco Bay delta, and arrived at the McCloud, fifty miles north of the nearest railhead in Red Bluff, in late summer. There the three encountered a band of Wintu natives still practicing their traditional fishery. In his reports to the USFC, he noted that the Indians were not particularly friendly: "[The] Indians had until this time succeeded in keeping the white man from their river with the exception of a Mr. Crooks, whom they murdered a week after I arrived."[6] Stone somehow overcame their hostility, however, and within two months not only had he and his two helpers hauled in enough materials to build the first rude salmon hatchery in California (through temperatures holding at 105 to 112 degrees), but he had convinced the Wintus to provide him with salmon brood stock on the condition that he return the meat of the fish once he had taken the eggs. The rough-hewn structure was named the Baird Hatchery, after its institutional benefactor.

(During Stone's first year in California, the great naturalist John Muir visited on one of his rambles through the country, and stayed long enough to lure the driven fish culturalist

to climb nearby Mt. Persephone with him. Muir left no rec-
ord of what he thought of Stone's manipulations of nature,
but he did note that the man's mountain-climbing stamina
was equal to his own.)

Stone was experiencing a taste of the North American
West that had assumed the proportions of a mythic Eden
back in the industrial East: place and human behavior still of
a piece, a remnant of the functional wild that still endured.
The encounter must have provoked some shock of recognition in him that went deeper than his utilitarian motivations.
In the thirty years that he made the Baird Hatchery his home
base, he would propound in his frequent reports to Washington, D.C., his belief that the presence of the native people was the definitive requirement for the survival of wild
salmon. Even as a witness and instrument of the Wintu people's last days, even as he propounded and actively pursued a
course of action that Alfred Crosby would come to call ecological imperialism, Stone held onto this intuitive grasp of
the relationship of local human behavior and salmon populations. In his 1873 report to the USFC, for instance, he wrote,

The supply of the Sacramento salmon has a singular natural protection arising from the fact that the McCloud River containing the
spawning grounds of these fish, is held entirely by Indians. . . . It
would be an inhuman outrage to drive this superior and inoffensive
race from the river, and I believe that the best policy to use with
them is to let them be where they are, and if necessary to protect
them from the encroachments of white men.[7]

In 1877, President Ulysses Grant established a 280-acre
federal reserve around the hatchery, and although he did so
not to protect the Indians but to safeguard the government's
investment, the garrison of soldiers established there did
seem to work at reducing friction between the indigenous inhabitants and the encroaching settlers. Stone himself drove

off one of the more insistent poachers (a man named Le-
chinsky), evidently with his fists, during the summer of his
honeymoon, in 1875 (a honeymoon spent, most typically,
at work).

Meanwhile, the Central Pacific Railroad was dynamiting
a right-of-way along the banks of the Sacramento, to complete a north-south line from San Francisco to Oregon. By
1883 the road crews had reached the mouth of the Pit River,
a few miles downstream from the Baird Hatchery, and created a barrier to the passage of fish up to the McCloud.
In August of 1883, Stone and his Wintu friends witnessed
a river barren of salmon in a reach where they had once
counted thousands of leapers in an hour.

However developed our empathic skills, the anguish of
one cannot be fully known by another; we can only imagine
the emotions and thoughts of the two groups of people on
encountering the empty river. The entrepreneurs from the
East must have suffered from the inexplicable failure of their
ambitions, must have lamented the fruit of their labor and
ideas wiped out in an instant. It is more difficult to imagine
the agony of the first peoples, for whom the life of the river
was an extension of existence. The USFC hatchery remained
closed for the next five years. For the Wintus this was the
end of a continuous history that stretched back thousands of
years.

Unfortunately, Livingston Stone's prescient insights
concerning the interrelationship between an inhabitory
people and the survival of wild fish stocks did little to temper
his enthusiasm for the promiscuous introduction of various
fishes from one place to another. By the time of the railway
disaster, the energetic Stone had extended his efforts far beyond the little hatchery on the McCloud, and his federal

funders had come to believe his work represented the wave
of the future.

In 1872 the entire start-up production of the McCloud
River hatchery was shipped east. Of fifty thousand fertilized
eggs taken, between two and three hundred survived the
torturous cross-country shipment by rail and were incubated to be released as fingerlings into the Susquehanna
River—never to be seen again. Neither the USFC's Spencer
Baird nor Stone himself were aware (nor would they have
thought it particularly noteworthy) that Atlantic salmon
were of a different genus than Pacific salmon, with significantly different life histories and environmental constraints.
For thirty years Livingston Stone would remain dedicated to
the idea that Pacific salmon eggs could be used to revive the
Atlantic salmon fishery, without a single incidence of success.[8]

In 1873 Stone traveled back East to supervise the conversion of a railway fruit car into an aquarium car, with tanks
cooled by ice and requiring frequent changes of water. The
car was loaded with three hundred thousand assorted fish—
including catfish, bullheads, trout, perch, bass, eels, and lob-
ster—for shipment to the West. Stone and his assistants rode
in the cold car, complaining of illness, and very nearly lost
their lives when a bridge collapsed under the weight of the
train, causing an inadvertent introduction of fish and fish
culturalists into the Elkhorn River of Nebraska. The latter
survived undaunted. In the same year, Stone received a shipment of Great Lakes whitefish, which he attempted, un-
successfully, to introduce into Clear Lake in northern California.

Later shipments from east to west included shad and
striped bass to be introduced into the Sacramento–San Joaquin system. One hundred and fifty striped bass planted in

the Carquinez Straits in 1879 were the seeds that grew into one of California's largest sport-fishing industries.[9] But striped bass aside, most of the exotic introductions disappeared without a trace. One "successful" introduction, the brown catfish, proliferated so rapidly that it drove the more valuable river perch and dace out of their ecological niches. By 1894, the *San Francisco Bulletin* would editorialize that "like the English sparrow [the catfish are] beyond extermination and are everywhere execrated."[10]

But Stone's most celebrated efforts were with the augmentation of chinook salmon populations in the Sacramento River. Within a few years of its founding, the Baird Hatchery had improved its techniques to the point where millions of eggs were being taken each year, and most of the hatched-out juveniles were being released into the Sacramento, which, then as now, was producing the largest part of the harvests of California's commercial salmon fishery. Ever-increasing annual catches were credited to Stone's efforts, overlooking the relevant fact that a burgeoning industry was putting more boats and more fishers in the waters each year.

Throughout his long and successful career as a promoter of salmon hatcheries, however, Stone worked from several disastrous misconceptions about the life histories of Pacific salmon, as did those who followed him.

Atlantic salmon, genus *Salmo*, like their Pacific cousins the steelhead, often survive their initial reproductive effort and return to the ocean for another year, then migrate back to the stream of their birth to spawn a second or even a third time, each time having grown larger and (in the case of females) capable of producing more eggs. However, both male and female Pacific salmon, genus *Oncorhynchus*—including sockeye, coho, and chinook (the latter also called king salmon)—always die after only one reproductive season. Stone's understanding of this phenomenon is unclear. It is hard to believe that he could have remained ignorant of this basic fact after working year after year with native runs of chinook. Joel Hedgpeth suggests that Stone, aware that most of the fish he was handling were three or four years old, speculated that they had spawned in other rivers before their final migration and death on the McCloud. Stone was evidently enough of a scientist to elevate experimental protocol over his own direct observation. Only in 1895, when Barton Evermann demonstrated conclusively in Idaho that chinook salmon perish after reproducing once, did Stone see fit to publish his own firsthand observations.[11]

This is a marvelous example of scientific protocol falling a generation or two behind the common sense of vernacular observation. The massive death of spawning populations of Pacific salmon produces one of the great spectacles of the river year as the dead adults drift against the banks of the river to decompose, drawing every carnivore and carrion-eater from within miles. The literature of exploration and settlement dating back to Lewis and Clark in 1803 is full of references to the stench and profligacy of windrows of dead fish rotting on the shores of salmon rivers. For its own reasons, however, the California Fish Commission preferred not to believe that Pacific salmon spawn only once. "If this were the fact," one commissioner is quoted as stating in 1876, "it would detract from their value,"[12] a telling pronouncement that illustrates both the Commission's perception of its own mission and the reciprocal and convolute relationship between science, commerce, and state regulation.

The second of Stone's misconceptions about the life histories of salmon—one that would not be corrected until long after his death in 1912, until after the Baird Hatchery closed forever in 1935—was pointed out by Joel Hedgpeth (who would go on to become one of California's most assertive advocates of environmental reform) in 1940:

> The principal basis for the assertions of the extravagant claims for the hatchery in its early years was the misconception of the efficiency of natural production, evidently based on nothing more than an *a priori* assumption that nature was inherently wasteful and inefficient. Stone in his first report, part of which consisted of answers to a series of questions written out by Professor Baird, wrote, "No one knows" opposite Baird's inquiry on the survival of naturally spawned eggs. At some time or another, he did dig in a nest, recovered some eggs and found but 8 per cent of them "vitalized." According to the 1878–79 Biennial Report of the California Fish Commission, "in a state of nature, only two eggs per thousand hatch." No authority is given for this interesting statement however. [13]

The climate of common wisdom prevailed, and gave Stone no reason to doubt that his (theoretically) higher rates of egg fertilization were an improvement on nature.

To his credit, Stone continuously pleaded for the budgeting of biologists into his program, but to no avail. It wasn't until 1937 that a New Zealand biologist, working with the offspring of naturalized salmon whose ancestors had come from the Baird Hatchery forty years earlier, determined that natural reproductive rates compared favorably with the success rates of hatcheries. [14] Later studies on Oregon's Kalama River found that trout spawned in the wild had three times the survival rate of hatchery-bred fish introduced into the same river. [15]

Finally, during Stone's career it was generally believed that salmon choose to reproduce in one river or another in a random fashion. It was not readily apparent that each glowing salmon egg contained within it a strategy for the survival of its species based on precise adaptation to the full range of environmental conditions its home stream might present during any one year—genetically encoded information that provided the skills for identifying the home stream along with a hardwired sense of the time when that particular stream would be at its optimal conditions for spawning. This was a concept counterintuitive to the new American mind, shaped as it had been by generations of restless wandering. Stone believed that salmon based their choice of reproductive sites entirely on the volume of water or "attraction flows" that might be present in one river or another at the time of the salmon's landward migration.

Stone, along with the state and industrial interests that enthusiastically embraced his hatchery strategies, remained unaware of more acute observations of the life history of salmon developing elsewhere in his own Euro-American cultural community. As early as 1880, A. C. Anderson, Inspector of Fisheries for British Columbia, had come to the conclusion that salmon were organized into discrete stocks rising out of specific waterways. Anderson seems to have based his conclusions on commonsense observations of the relationship between numbers of parent spawners in a particular river with the number of returning adults a generation later.[16] He and his successor, John Peace Babcock, were successful in establishing discrete watershed-based stocks as the basis for British Columbia salmon fishery management. Today their decisions are reflected in a salmon fishery that remains more vital than those of its neighbors to the south.

Over fifty years after Anderson's work, Willis Rich, a biologist working as chief of research for the Oregon Fish Commission, would conduct a ten-year study, published in 1939, that came to the same conclusions, which Rich called the home stream theory. And Willis Rich was not afraid to spell out the implications of his conclusions for fisheries management:

Given a species which is broken up into a number of such isolated groups or populations, it is obvious that the conservation of the species as a whole resolves into the *conservation of every one of the component groups;* that the success of efforts to conserve the species will depend, not only on the results attained with any one population, but on a fraction of the total number of individuals in the species that is contained within the populations affected by the conservation measure. [Emphasis added.][17]

In other words, the health and viability of the species depends on the maintenance of its home-stream diversity, and by implication on the preservation of the spawning and rearing habitats of those home streams. But Rich's work came too late to have an immediate influence on the momentum that hatchery technology had gained by this time.

By 1978, California commercial salmon fisheries, along with those of most of the Pacific Northwest, had become dependent on the annual flood of juvenile fish pumped into rivers by various hatcheries. Since 1872, well over a hundred and fifty salmon hatcheries had come and gone, built by state and federal agencies or by individuals. As the waters of Western rivers were incrementally appropriated in the service of development, each new damming scheme tended to include the construction of a salmon hatchery to serve an increasingly international market for salmon flesh. By the beginning of the 1970s, 95 percent of California's spawning habitat had either been degraded by development, logging, or mining, or had been eliminated altogether by the hundreds of dams built for irrigation or power generation. In response, the state had gradually assumed control of hatchery culture, and hatchery programs had become the foundation for the rationalization of state salmon management. As the technology of artificial propagation had improved and cost-benefit analyses had been applied, California's hatchery program had been consolidated into nine centralized facilities, eight of them associated with mitigation for the destruction of freshwater habitat by dams.

Salmon stocks were still being transferred opportunistically from drainage to drainage. Salmon eggs from Puget Sound and Alaska had been used to kick-start California hatcheries; California-born fry were introduced into rivers draining into Puget Sound. Nearly half of the salmon production on the Sacramento River, which accounts for three-quarters of California's commercial catch, originates in hatcheries. The salmon runs on the second greatest river in California, the San Joaquin, had for the purposes of the commercial fisheries been extirpated. And because of the pervasiveness and promiscuity of hatchery introductions, the genetic composition of all of the Pacific salmon species was tending toward homogenization.

No one knew with any exactitude just what was being lost, but common sense and the home stream theory (by this time widely known in the scientific and fishing community) led to at least two tentative conclusions. The first of these was that the hatchery management habit of introducing stocks from one river into another, a practice which had led to interbreeding, had also led to a demonstrable loss of successful adaptive response to variations in water flow and other physical changes in the fishes' natal streams. Certainly of equal importance, but more speculative, was the possibility that the species strategy of adaptation to specific waterways included a variable range of resistance to any of several diseases that could strike a particular waterway or wider areas of the Pacific itself. If a wild or introduced pathogen were to wipe out the salmon stock on any one river, that river over time might gradually become recolonized by strays from another stock, homogenized or not. (From a hatchery manager's perspective, such an occurrence could be seen as merely a technical challenge: the disappeared population could simply be *replaced* by pumping the damaged river full of generic hatchery salmon.) But what if a foreign pathogen were to strike the mixed populations while the salmon were swimming freely in the ocean where they spend the greater part of their lives? A homogenized species would lack the variations in natural resistance that logic would lead one to expect in a more diverse population. New fish diseases had already begun to appear with alarming regularity in more contained fisheries like those in Puget Sound, spread either by hatchery fish whose resistance had been reduced by the stress of high population density in hatchery rearing situations or by fish escaped from commercial experiments with Norwegian stock in the waters of Puget Sound and British Columbia. Local population crashes had resulted. It was not such a long leap of the imagination to project a much larger tragic scenario in which a pathogen could sweep through an entire species during its free-swimming residence in the Pacific and decimate it. Given this scenario, the few wild strains remaining scattered through the Pacific Northwest might be the only hope for the survival of the species.

Anthropologist Clifford Geertz cautions us that "if you want to understand what a science is, you should look in the first instance not at its theories or its findings, and certainly not at what its apologists say about it; you should look at what its practitioners do."[18] The same observation holds true in the biological and physical sciences. Until as recently as fifteen years ago, mainstream fisheries biology had put itself at the service of the utilitarian motives of the society of which it was a part. Dan Bottom, a biologist for the Oregon Department of Fish and Wildlife, would write in 1996 that "the early fish culture movement formed the foundation upon which applied fisheries science was built."[19] In fact, somewhere along the line, the American Fish Culturists' Association changed its name to the American Fisheries Society. (It should be noted, also, that over the past decade this organization—still the leading professional organization of fisheries biologists—has come to be among the most vigorous advocates of the home stream theory and the preservation and restoration of native stocks, a hopeful indication of shifting priorities in the larger culture.)

Hatchery culture served the purposes of its clients—government and industry. In turn, hatchery culture became the dominant client of fisheries biology. The parameters of research projects came to be determined by the goals of hatcheries. Fisheries science developed not as a study of the habits of wild fish, but put itself from its beginnings at the service of the domestication of those fish.

Hatchery-dominated fisheries science also fit right in with the whole huge range of large-scale projects being applied to the Western landscape during the same period. Engineers building dams for irrigation and power generation, for instance, could always point to the installation of a hatchery as environmental mitigation. The declining health of waterways could be dismissed by the professional foresters designing the operations of a burgeoning timber industry.

Expert panels regulating ocean fishery quotas would come to use hatchery releases as baseline figures for predicting ocean abundance. Hatcheries made possible a self-sustaining feedback loop that justified the existence of state regulatory agencies. The large numbers of hatchery fish released each year (over three million in 1978) maintained the illusion of natural abundance for the clients of the agencies—the commercial and recreational fishers close up, and the consuming public in the middle distance. The license fees paid by the both commercial and recreational fishers supported the introduction of ever more hatchery fish. The problems of domestication and simplification of genetic diversity—if these issues were raised at all—appeared to be secondary worries that a little more science would surely resolve.

Despite the fact that salmon populations continued their precipitous rate of decline during exactly the same period that production of artificially propagated fish was increasing exponentially, very few stopped to consider that hatcheries might be part of the problem. The system had been successful in maintaining the spectacle of natural provision for a consumer public that had little interest in the place-specific origins of canned salmon with a shelf-life of years, fresh-frozen fish, or even the delectable lox available for a price on either coast of North America. Pen-raised salmon from Norway was beginning to flood the North American fresh fish market, and few consumers could tell the difference. Of those who could, even fewer cared.

As early as the 1880s, isolated voices from commercial fishers, industrial cannery operators, and a few scientists had been sounding the alarm about the decline of salmon populations, and many of those who spoke up recognized the role that the degradation of freshwater habitat played in that decline. Since the publication of Rich's study in the 1930s, an increasing number of scientists had also become concerned about the damage being done to naturally reproducing native populations by hatcheries. But these voices had not been able to cut through the illusion of abundance that anyone could see in the supermarket. To raise the issue of protecting wild salmon, as activists like Bill Bakke were beginning to do in

Oregon, was like criticizing the acrobat's costume from the edge of a very well-attended and satisfying circus. We were proposing a solution before the problem had been clearly articulated.

"How can salmon be endangered when you can buy them in cans in supermarkets?" asked Idaho Congressional Representative Helen Chenowith as recently as 1996. Although the sweeping national environmental legislation of the early seventies was widely popular, very few people connected ideas about the preservation of the wild with the food that appeared on their supper tables, or indeed, with any other aspect of their daily lives. Wild was a nice place to visit and we certainly wanted some left for our children, but for most people it had not a whole lot to do with daily life.

The eighteenth-century ideal of independent and self-reliant agricultural production that had inspired the early fish culturalists had been subsumed by the dominant artifact of the nineteenth century in America, the factory system. Hatchery technology had become an integral part of the commodification of rivers, the process that historian Richard White describes as the transformation of rivers into "organic machines."[20] In a century, hatchery science had effectively isolated salmon from their habitats, and consumers of salmon from the knowledge of their wild provenance. Management depending on such science had driven stock after stock to the brink of extinction. Livingston Stone's enthusiasms had grown beyond anything he could possibly have imagined.

A hundred years after Stone's arrival in the West, few salmon rivers had been spared the introduction of hatchery-bred fish. When our little cadre on the Mattole gathered together the thin files of state data on the river, we made the startling discovery that the Mattole sheltered a strain of native king salmon not crossed with hatchery introductions. (The only introduction of hatchery kings had occurred in 1938, when a single desultory release of fewer than five thousand kings and one thousand cohos had been dumped into the upper reaches of the river. But the number of fish was too small, and had happened too long ago, to have had much ecological consequence.)

From our perspective, in 1980, this discovery took our ambitions for the preservation and restoration of the river out of the realm of the provincial; it gave them evolutionary significance. Further research revealed that the Mattole's was one of only half a dozen isolated populations of salmon in California that retained a native intelligence that had not been dumbed down by interbreeding with hatchery fish. The recovery and maintenance of the king salmon in our little coastal river was now more than a neighborhood issue. The long-term survival of the species could depend on the genetic variations encoded in the few remaining wild gene pools.

*There is presently no other way for humans to
educate themselves for survival and fulfillment than
through the instruction available from the natural world.*

THOMAS BERRY, *Dream of the Earth*

A RACE OF SALMON is an expression of the river, the
intelligence of the terrestrial home traveled to far seas—always to return to its place of birth. Salmon return to their
riverine homes with the wealth of the great sea embodied in
nutrients they will deliver to the waters and the plants and
animals of the forest at the completion of their lives. Migration is an adaptation toward abundance: more fish are born
in a river than the river can support; thus out-migration to
the pastures of the sea. In the case of salmonids, migration
and return is a dynamic ritual binding population to place.
Each salmon species is divided into hundreds of distinctive
stocks, races that can breed with each other but which develop different behavioral and physical characteristics over
time: larger and smaller sizes, different timing regimens
based on the time of year their freshwater homes will swell
to a volume large enough to carry them up to their spawning
grounds. People who have fished the sea for years off the

abundant coasts of British Columbia and Alaska will swear that they can detect differences in the flavor of the meats of the various stocks, and will develop gourmet preferences for the flesh of one run over another.

The stock of fish that has adapted to the Mattole River, as I've noted, has information coded in its genes that impels it to seek out home waters in the fall. As with most small coastal rivers at these latitudes, a bar will have formed across the mouth of the Mattole to block migration of fish in or out between the months of June and October. But by Halloween, in a year of average rainfall, two or three storms will have each released an inch or more of rain into the system. The berm between freshwater and salt becomes more narrow as the river rises behind it, and it trembles under foot. Then the river will have developed enough volume and force to blow through the sand bar that the winds and tides have been building and rebuilding all summer.

Some version of sea lion heaven is occurring just offshore: the salmon have arrived and are waiting for the berm to break. The fish are at the prime of their lives, fat and firm of flesh. They will never be better as food, be you human or sea mammal. The lions and seals roll in the surf and take a bite here and there, a demonstration of the profligacy of nature that leaves some human fishers furious: the prime salmon killed by a single bite out of its vital center and left for the gulls and mergansers. When the bar finally breaks it may be the result of trickling erosion, a passage a day in the making, or it may happen in a matter of minutes as the cohesion holding the grains together fails and a great chunk of sand disintegrates all at once, suddenly liquified.

Salmon leave the rivers where they were born and spend most of their lives, one to seven years depending on species, traveling in great circles around portions of the North Pacific

before making a beeline toward their home river for their
one chance at reproduction. In general, Asian salmon make
their circular journey traveling in a clockwise direction,
North American salmon counter-clockwise, all headed toward the food-rich waters of the North Pacific and Aleutian
seas. They travel enormous distances, distances that would
leave a human being hopelessly lost without a compass or
more sophisticated navigational aids. Yet they return to their
natal streams to spawn with exacting regularity.

How do they do it? To put it simply, we don't know.
Salmon, individually or collectively, find their way back
home through mechanisms of which we have little understanding.

The fact that salmon usually take a different route home
than they took on their outward voyage would seem to eliminate the notion that individual salmon might *remember* their
way back. Various stocks of Fraser River salmon have been
observed to take different routes home on different years, ap-
parently depending on water temperatures and food concentrations during the previous winter. After a warm winter,
when ocean nutrient concentrations have moved north,
salmon will find their way back to the Fraser around the
northern end of Vancouver Island. After a colder winter, the
route is more likely to be through the Strait of Juan de Fuca,
at the southern end of the island. Even if memory were the
mechanism that explained the phenomenon, it would be a
startling accomplishment, comparable to you or me walking
across North America and remembering our way back over
the same route. As a person of some local fame for getting
lost in my own two-square-mile home watershed, I have no
doubt what disastrous confusions would encumber me were
I to take on a trek of a scale comparable to the Pacific salmon's
voyage, even though I have the comparative advantage of the

enormous variety and particularity of the terrestrial landscape. What markers exist in a thousand fathoms of sea water?

Orientation clues *do* exist in the aquatic vastness. Their existence, if not their nature, is demonstrated annually by the return of the salmon through thousands of miles of what is to us featureless brine. Salmon perceptors function so differently from ours that we are only able to think about them through metaphorical references to our own repertoire of technological inventions of relatively recent vintage, like the clock and the compass, or those of more ancient provenance like the calendar and the map. (Humans have invented many of these wonderful tools specifically to deal with the problem of crossing the seemingly featureless oceans that make up the largest part of the Earth's surface.) Scientists attempting to grapple with the vastness of the waters *beneath* the surface, a vastness that is overwhelmingly larger than all terrestrial landscapes put together, have been forced to rely on these tools as metaphors for salmon sentience. "Every salmon," the fisheries biology instructor will tell you, "has an innate compass, calendar, map, and clock."

But salmon *don't* have tools. Salmon swim in a living medium full of the buzz and pulse of electromagnetic fields and currents, within infinitesimal differences in temperature and salinity and light and food. Populations of Bristol Bay sockeye salmon marked and observed over a twenty-three-hundred-mile range extending from the Gulf of Alaska to the western subarctic Pacific have turned up at the mouths of their natal streams within three days of each other, a phenomenon biologists accept as evidence that individual salmon *navigate*—that is to say, each fish is somehow able to determine its position at sea and choose a direct path to its natal stream. But theirs is a different sort of navigation than tool-using humans practice. It is as if you or I were transported while we slept to an unknown location thousands of miles from our home. Waking up naked, we would feel the electromagnetism and the anomalies of gravity through the soles of our feet, smell the air and analyze it with our skin, watch the clouds and the angle of the sun, pick subtle messages out of the wind and the sound it makes passing through trees we hadn't seen before, point ourselves in a direction and walk straight home. Or rather trot home: those sockeyes mentioned earlier moved at an average speed of thirty miles a day.[1]

Reductionist science attempts to understand the lives of salmon in separation from their field of being, the living sea. And we don't have the intellectual or perceptual tools to do more than begin to consider the complexity of the web of interactions in a milieu so different from our own. That's fine with me: I can imagine the mystery of salmon as a field of creative interaction rather than a stubborn obstacle to our "understanding" them.

Over the past two decades, the disappearance of Pacific salmon populations in the southern reaches of their range has created a new generation of passionate biologists who seem ready to embrace the fecund tension contained in recognition of the limits of rationality. Willa Nehlson, one of the most hard-working and effective members of this cohort, writes,

Some things about salmon we do understand or come close to understanding. Others lie within reach and require only more time, more cultural and scientific advancement, perhaps more humility. But much remains that we cannot easily understand, will have to stretch ourselves to grasp, and may still fail to comprehend. Then we will have to be content with articulating the questions or failing that, struggling with a sense of mystery.[2]

The word *empathy* comes from a Latin word meaning to suffer with gathered senses, and empathy is the human skill that recombines the elements of life that Western science has so thoroughly reduced to its component parts. Empathy with lives that are alien to our own is the human impulse that gives rise to vernacular practices that celebrate and regulate our links to other species.

If our engagement with natural processes is beyond our ability to measure and quantify in the laboratory, it may be that the only way to immerse ourselves in those processes is through the long practice of cumulative attentiveness. In the close-mouthed world of reciprocal perception, there is no way to learn to live in place but from the place itself. Even the waters can teach us, if we can quiet our appetite for "rational" explanation. One of the few documented interviews with first peoples of the Mattole gives us this:

Among the Mattole, conduct toward waves is prescribed: The water watches you and has a definite attitude, favorable or otherwise, toward you. Do not speak just before a wave breaks. Do not speak to passing rough water in a stream. Do not look at water very long for any one time, unless you have been to this spot ten times or more.

Then the water there is used to you and does not mind if you're looking at it. Older men can talk in the presence of the water because they have been about so long that the water knows them. Until the water at any spot does know you, however, it becomes very rough if you talk in its presence or look at it too long.[3]

And if it is salmon that chooses to lead some of us back to our immersion in the natural world, then our first order of business must be the survival of salmon, the health of the waters.

Morning of the fifth day of the calendar year 1983. We are at the place we call Arcanum, after the name of the business run by the two potters who own the land. They have given the same name to the little stream that runs though the shaded glade where our incubation and rearing setup has been built. Twice each day for the next two months, in whatever weather, John or Greg will leave their work in the potting shed to scramble down the steep quarter-mile path to the glade. They will backtrack up the little feeder creek to the two spring boxes that provide the water that keeps the eggs alive and developing. They will make sure nothing has clogged the line, will flush the filters built from fifty-gallon drums. They will note the temperature and flow, check for any fungi that might be growing among the eggs in the incubation trough. If they see anything alarming, they will get on the telephone to Gary, who will be on call for these two months.

For the first month, the eggs will sit in the trough, in baskets made from plastic mesh and clotheshanger wire, each basket containing the offspring of a single adult female. At this stage of development, the eggs are so fragile that a sharp blow to the plywood trough could damage them. John or Greg will raise and lower the padlocked lid as quietly and carefully as if they were art thieves in a museum at night. Once the fetus within each egg develops an eye large enough to be apparent through the translucent shell, the eggs will have toughened enough so that they can be moved to the nearby hatchbox.

This morning a translucent layer of mist lies over the length of the receding river like thin white cream on the dirty coffee of the water just below. Occasional turbulence in the water sends a shredded column of mist floating up to the tops of the redwoods, where it hangs and swirls until it is dissipated by a bright, almost warm sun. The moisture in the air both softens and intensifies the light; the day envelops us like a great, moist, green bud unfolding.

Biologist Gary moves about as briskly as any surgeon, mildly impatient with the random movements of the rest of us. Gary will have spent hours yesterday making lists and gathering gear for the job at hand. Now he is laying it out just so. The five-gallon white plastic buckets to receive the eggs sit in a row on the ground; the little bags of local anesthetic and the clever hatchery knives, razor-sharp little sickles attached to a plastic ring to fit around a finger, are laid out on a knocked-together bench beside rolls of paper towels and a length of surgical tubing. A fisherman's scale sits next to a yardstick borrowed from someone's sewing kit back home. Gary makes notes in a yellow Write-in-the-Rain notebook with one of the several mechanical pencils he has stuck in various pockets of his surveyor's vest: air temperature, high and low water temperatures as measured by the Minimax thermometer suspended in the river by a cord.

David moves restlessly among us with his usual slightly distracted courtliness, inquiring about our families, about news of the river and the weather and local gossip. His questions are full of kind concern, but his attention drifts if the answers are over-long. One moment Stevie is excitedly describing the adventures of the new year. Then he is pacing a little apart from the group, muttering to himself the drill of the work to come. I am fiddling with an ironwood killing club, a short length of wood so dense it will not float. It is ornately carved, a gift from an Alaska fishing partner years before. I only barely hear the conversation around me.

Each of us has performed this rite a number of times before, but it never ceases to be weighted with nearly intolerable significance, the irreducible requirement to do it right.

A small galvanized stock-watering tank sits on the ground; we busy ourselves bucketing water up from the river to fill it. Everything is ready. Gary measures a few teaspoons of the anesthetic into the tank. We have been told the white powder resembles xylocaine, the same stuff the dentist swabs on your gums to numb them in preparation for the injection of novocaine. Stevie, nearly dancing with anticipation, runs to the holding tank once Gary tells him we are ready, lifts the New Year's female out of the water in her tube, and rushes her down to the drugged water in the stock tank. Once there, the staccato sound of her tail beating against the white tube slows to stillness. With no wasted movement, Gary pulls the cotter pin that holds the end of the tube closed, reaches in with one hand and lifts the great fish out of the water by her tail. Using two hands now, he holds her, head down, at arm's length away from himself.

I have handed the ironwood club to Stevie. By some unspoken calculation, it's his turn. Stevie holds the club over his shoulder with both hands. He is coiled tightly like a baseball batter at plate; he squints at the fish with his one good eye. It will be a mutual embarrassment if it takes him more than one blow to kill her. The club comes around at the same time as he is taking two quick steps toward Gary and the salmon, and it connects solidly at the back of her head, just behind her eyes. She shudders for a moment and is still. Stevie drops the club in the grass.

"Good," Gary murmurs, "good."

Then he slides one hand down the fish's sleek body to bring her head up almost parallel to the ground, careful to keep her tail elevated slightly with his other hand, so no eggs will spill onto the ground. He hands her to David, who waits while I scramble for one of the white buckets. Each of us is muttering cautionary instructions to the others, *careful, careful, head down, head up, don't drop her now.* No one hears. We have moved beyond our nervous ambivalence at the arrogance of our intention and are wholly occupied by the ritual. Gary is drying the fish now with paper towels—no water or slime can touch the eggs before they are mixed with the males' milt. Stevie is trotting up the slope once more to move the two males into the drug tank.

By the time the males have quieted down, Gary has finished his tender cleaning. He slides the spawning knife over his middle finger, with the little sickle blade pointed outward. Even after three years, it is rare for Gary the biologist to entrust this part of the ceremony to another of us. He inserts the tip of the curved blade an eighth of an inch into the opening called the vent, on the underside of the female salmon near her tail, taking care to cut nothing but the wall of the stomach muscle. He jerks the knife upward in firm inch-long strokes. We have fallen so silent now that we can hear the crunch of the knife slicing through muscle at each stroke. At the first cut, eggs begin to cascade into the bucket I am holding up beside the fish's tail, close beneath the vent. The eggs pour out, each short stroke of the knife releasing more.

The morning is bright but each translucent egg seems to glow brighter as if lit by a light from within. Gary ends his cut at the sternum of the fish, puts the knife aside, and reaches up into the open cavity to break loose any eggs still clinging within. He allows himself a small expression of pride at his judgment: "All ripe, every one of 'em ripe. I'll bet she's carrying more than four thousand."

The males are floating on their sides in the drugged water of the stock tank. David lifts one of them out belly up, the head of the fish cradled inside one elbow, its tail held tight in his hand. I support the fish's back while I wipe him clean with another length of paper towels. David massages the belly of the fish between fingers and thumb, with several firm strokes down toward the vent. A clear liquid jets from the vent onto the ground. As soon as the discharge turns milky, David holds the vent of the male over the bucket with the eggs while I hold the tail off to the side. An ounce or two of milt squirts into the bucket and the coelemic fluid surrounding the eggs turns cloudy. While Stevie returns the first male to clean water, we repeat the process with the second one. Afterward, I lower the fingers of one hand into the heart of creation and stir it once, twice. For a moment my mind is completely still. Am I holding my breath? I am held in the thrall of a larger sensuality that extends beyond the flesh.

By the time I have lifted my fingers out of the bucket, fertilization will have taken place or not. Clean water is now dribbled into the bucket through the surgical tubing. This will cause the single opening in each egg to close. Within an hour the eggs will have developed membranes strong enough to allow them to be moved gently to the incubation trough.

There is a flurry of busyness as Stevie watches to be sure the males revive in the fresh water. Gary weighs and measures the body of the female, makes notations, and returns her to the river where her carcass will contribute to the nutrient cycle that will in time nourish young fish. Then we sit quietly to wait for the eggs to harden. No one has much to say. Each of us sits or paces or smokes, each strays over to the white bucket now and then to stare into it. A little congratulatory *hey!* will come from one or the other of us: we have not done too badly today.

There is a hard knot of relationship in the act of killing a creature of another species. It is an act that dissolves the illusion of individuality, of separateness. Perhaps this explains the terror that attends each such occasion, the awe that has inspired rituals and regulations, ceremonies and prayers in all human cultures throughout the ages. We are reminded in the most immediate way of our own mortality, an idea with which we may or may not have come to terms.

Perhaps this explains the distracted nervousness of our particular group earlier, our quiet introspection now. Modernity has distanced us from wild reality so that when it comes to killing and dying, each of us must deal with the mystery of it alone and uneasy. But the meaning persists in experiences of killing and dying, beyond cultural interpretation. The lesson of interpenetration is always available to us, regardless of our cultural conditioning. It is also a lesson we humans seem to be increasingly happy to ignore as we allow distant and abstract economic institutions to disguise and conceal the relationship. Could the food we buy in pretty shrink-wrapped packages ever have been alive as we are alive?

I am thinking now, on this morning, of a moment in my life ten years past, a moment that I have never fully comprehended. It was my second or third day out of Ketchikan Alaska as crew on a salmon purse seiner.

In the Pacific Northwest, the purse seine has its origins in prehistory, in long, shallow nets made from twine woven painstakingly from the fiber of wild iris leaves, from cedar bark, from wild hemp, from willow bark. These nets, with a smaller mesh than others used to entangle the gills of fish, might be sixty to a hundred and fifty feet long, six to twenty feet deep. Making such a net was a communal endeavor that must have taken weeks, months: fibers no longer than the length of a forearm were twisted into long loops of cord, which were then woven and tied into large nets with an exactly measured mesh. (The knot used to tie the mesh five thousand years ago is the same one used today, the ubiquitous sheetbend.) One end of the net was anchored to shore in deep but quiet waters. The other end was towed out by a canoe, then towed back to shore to form a circle. The net was weighted with rocks to hold down its bottom while wooden floats kept its top edge on the surface of the water. As the ends of the net were pulled ashore the circle became ever more constricted and the fish crowded within it were delivered to fishers with dip nets or spears. Versions of this sort of beach seine are still used by subsistence fishers in the inland waterways of British Columbia and Alaska.

With the arrival of the Euro-American commercial fishery in northwest North America, the old technology was adapted to deeper water, and eventually to diesel-powered boats. The nets, constructed now by clever machines, have grown to a quarter of a mile long and fifty feet deep. Polystyrene floats and lead-weighted lines have replaced wood and stone. Brass rings were added to the bottom of the net, through which a line is passed. The net is towed into its pretty circle by a skiff only slightly less powerful than the mother ship. Then, when the line running through the rings at the bottom of the net is winched on board, it closes off the whole expanse of water inside the net, along with all the life within it—like the drawstrings on a pouch, the purse seine.

For many years, the large nets were then drawn on board the mother boats by men straining with all their strength against the weight and pull of the water. (To the deckhands, it can't have seemed much of an improvement over the older native practices, which in my mind I see as leisurely and festive events.) In the days before sonar fish-finders and carefully coded radio transmissions, finding the schools of salmon that triggered the setting of the net depended on the hard-earned skills of the skipper, skills based on experience and observation. It was a calling to which the best of them devoted a life. Experience taught them a sense of timing that combined the day of the year with water temperatures and local weather patterns. Anomalies in the way sea mammals and birds were acting were a language they learned to understand; a boil of herring or a congregation of birds spoke to them more clearly than did their wives on the too-rare occasions when they returned home.

The perfect set enclosed a few thousand acre-feet of water swarming with schools of salmon—innumerable small pink salmon, their numbers compensating for the low price dictated by their eventual processing into canned food for pets and poor people; chinooks, less abundant but huge, and cohos, sleek and firm, which brought a better price and were headed for regional dinner tables. The great prize was the beautiful red-fleshed sockeye, prime food delivered fresh or frozen to expensive restaurants in distant capitals.

By 1973, an innovation had been added to purse-seine technology that increased its efficiency enormously—the power gurdy. A gurdy is a stationary pulley hung on a davit. On salmon trollers, which catch fish by hook and line, the davit holds the pulley out over the water away from the boat, to provide smooth passage for the fishing lines when they are being pulled in or let out by hand, or by hydraulically powered winches. On a purse seiner, the power gurdy is a large, hydraulically powered hard rubber reel, hung by steel beams twelve feet above the stern of the boat, large and powerful enough to haul in both ends of the purse seine and drop them onto the net platform below.

Now the net, weighing several tons, could be pulled on board mechanically, the large winch started and stopped by a remote push-button. The time it took to play out the net and pull it in was reduced to half an hour, increasing the number of sets that one crew could make in a day by a factor of four or more. The work of the crew changed from two hours of long, slow pulling to ten minutes of frenzy for a stern crew of three whose job it was to stack the incoming net under our feet at the same time as it was descending on our heads. We worked in full raingear with our sleeves and pantslegs taped shut against the stinging jellyfish and the enormous amounts of water. The occasional smaller gill-entangled fish was ignored.

The independent skippers of these fishing boats had embraced the new machinery as the promise of their own survival in the fiercely competitive race to catch enough fish each year to make payments on the expensive new gear, to make mortgage payments on the house on shore, to keep food on the table for the kids. The new gear allowed them to catch more fish; the expense of the new gear *required* them to catch more fish. They were like caged squirrels on an exercise wheel.

For the crewman, the first challenge of the new machinery was simply to survive it. We were driven by the speed at which the power gurdy poured the bulk of the net down upon us. We worked in short bursts of incredible effort. It was the four-hundred-yard dash of fishing. We couldn't have moved any faster than the inexorable turn of the gurdy pushed us, and had the net been fifty feet longer it would have been an effort beyond our endurance. I was thirty-five years old, the oldest green member of the crew by a good ten years. The younger men on either side of me were of the type that rises full-hearted to challenges to their strength and stamina. Like athletes, they turned the challenge into art, a wild muscular dance. For my part, I thought only of trying to keep up with the younger men. The crew on the stern gave all their concentration and strength to meeting the demands of the machine. Sticks and twigs must be removed so as not to foul the net when racing to make the next set; if the power gurdy had to be stopped to remove debris, the skipper might fly into a rage. Keeping pace with the speed at which the seine came on board would for ten or fifteen minutes occupy every corner of consciousness, every fiber of muscle.

The moment of truth at the end of each set comes when the pocket at the bottom of the purse has been drawn in close to the boat, the remainder of the net stacked on board. If the men on the stern, the web-men, have performed well, this will be the first time the power gurdy has paused in its relentless turning. Now the whole crew—all seven of us—rushes to the side to see the size of the catch. Each one of us hopes to see the frenzied boil in the water that will tell us the catch is a big one, the payload that will make our day or our week. With the whine of the power winch stilled, the idling engine of the boat and the raucous scream of gulls are background noises that frame a moment frozen in time. The bunched floats bob and drift in the swell. Someone will break the curious stillness with a shout of "Payload!" if the net's pocket is full, or "Water haul" if, as happens more frequently, it is empty. Most often, twenty to a hundred salmon of various sizes circle languidly within the enclosure. One or another of them will be charging the seine, searching for a way out of the strange obstacle that has interrupted its migration. The net is full of motion and life; it is a cell isolated suddenly from the living plasm of the sea.

Two or three of the crew hold the top edges of the seine up out of the water with long boat hooks, an occasionally successful attempt to keep the jumpers inside. Two more gather the seine at the level of the rail and tie it tight with a line that is attached to a separate winch that will lift the bottom of the net with its captured fish on board. The power winch whines again, and the writhing cell of web and fish is hauled over the deck, pouring a ton of sea water as it comes up and is muscled on board.

A trip-line opens the purse, and the load of fish falls to the deck. They flop and writhe noisily, their tails pounding against the wooden deck. They are ignored or kicked aside as preparations for the next set are made. (Only after the net is ready to be deployed into the water once more will a large hatch in the center of the stern deck be lifted so the fish can be put into the hold. They take a long time to die down there. Often, while we are hosing down the deck to clear it of seaweed and jellyfish, and the bolder seagulls are making runs at the flotsam, we can hear the fish drumming themselves to death below our feet, the sound amplified by the echo in the mostly empty space.)

In retrospect, I can see that we were a perfect microcosm of an extractive industrial economy. The cannery owned and maintained the boat, which was leased to the skipper. The skipper owned the huge web of net, which had to be repaired daily and replaced entirely every two years or so at a cost of several thousand dollars. Boat, net, skipper, and crew each were recompensed by a share of the profits from the catch after fuel and food expenses had been taken off the top. Our livelihoods depended entirely on the size of the season's catch, and it was not impossible to work for four months of intermittent twenty-hour days and find oneself broke at the end of the fishing year. Each one of us was unthinkingly married to the goal of taking all the fish we could in the shortest time possible, and the pace and practice of our work was determined by the machinery we used.

Under such conditions, the nature of what we were doing—taking life in order to feed ourselves—became obscure, if not lost altogether. We could not afford to see the creatures dying slowly on the deck and in the fish hold as manifestations of creation equal in complexity and vitality to ourselves. We could only allow ourselves to see the salmon as objects, as product, a product that we hoped would allow us to pay the rent at home for a little longer than the duration of the fishing season.

This conditioning was reinforced by a collective psychology in the social pressure cooker of seven men isolated on a fifty-foot boat. It was a taboo all the stronger for remaining unspoken that the death of the fish was not to be discussed. Perhaps *taboo* is the wrong word, coming to us as an anglicized version of a Tongan word which can be translated as sacred. But the economic objectification of what we were doing was, in fact, violating something in us that does lie in the realm of the sacred: individuality disappears except as it can be defined in relation to the whole. By denying ourselves the perception of our relation to the creatures dying on deck we were in some essential way denying ourselves a wholeness of being. And that knowledge lay large and dark and unarticulated just below the limited range of expression our condition allowed.

For non-Indian Americans too new to the land and waters of the Pacific Northwest to have developed ceremonies of place, the messages that salmon bring us are the same messages they have always brought, but they are not heard by most of us. Now—*here*—the message of the wild is fairly screaming at us in the midst of a deckload of slowly dying fish, but the message is carried at a different frequency than the one pulsing between the twin poles of our modern cultural icons of property and individualism. All of us on the boat speak English, and among us there is a smattering too of Norwegian, of Czech, of German—all languages which have been twisted over time into compliance with the dictates of economics and the physical sciences. None of us knows a word of Tlingit or Haida or Salish, languages that still resonate with the lives of salmon. Nevertheless, each of us retains some genetic memory—a memory imbedded in our flesh—of the wild relationships out of which we have evolved. The demands of the power gurdy rob us of all but a dim and paradoxical remnant of direct engagement with the

processes of life, with the genteel ethic of the clean kill—
the expression of respect and compassion that recognizes the
relationship between eater and eaten.

On the day I am thinking of, the lines have been carefully
coiled and the stacked web checked to make sure it will flow
out smoothly during the next set; the skiff is snubbed up
close to the mother ship. The diesels roar at full bore as we
take a position among the other purse seine boats to wait for
the next set. Only now are the fish on deck given attention.
Most of them are still vigorously alive, struggling and flop-
ping against the alien media of full light and air. The crew
react variously to the prospect of turning flesh into product.
Some have leaped forward in their minds and are already cal-
culating pounds and translating them into dollars; they do
their work gleefully, shouting happily. Others sweep the fish
into the hold tight-jawed and silent. One, a college boy/
naturalist, had signed on to get close to ocean life-forms. Although no one has told him so, he knows as well as anyone
that he dare not take the time to dispatch the fish respectfully
and individually. He seems to go crazy, kicking the fish and
shouting curses at them. I notice that he seems to be aiming
the kicks of his steel-toed rubber boots at that spot behind
the head of each fish that will kill it quickly.

I have no memory of having arrived where I did by any logical thought process; I don't remember telling myself that
this is what I should do. But I found myself alone in a dark
corner of the fish hold squatting with a ten- or twelve-pound
sockeye salmon still alive across my knees. With a knife I
opened up its chest cavity just enough to find the heart and
tear it out with two fingers and a thumb. It came with a ripping and squirting sound. I popped the heart into my mouth
and bit down once, hard, through the gristly thing. One bite
brought a flavor like all of Icy Straits and enough saliva to

float ten salmon hearts, enough to swallow it whole. As I swallowed, all my floating terrors gained a name and swept through me with the intensity of a hurricane. Fear of fish flesh and cold blood, fear of slime on the flesh of fish and its absence on the skin of snakes, fear of the strangeness of other species, fear of a world barren of human thought, fear of death: my own and all of it.

I was back on the deck minutes later; no one seemed to have noticed my absence. I resumed the drill of preparing for the next set with an unusual clarity of vision and emptiness of mind. The shards of light reflecting from the surrounding sea, the crazy screams of the gulls and terns, the fading colors of the dying fish, all took on the aspect of a single thought that may or may not have been my own.

Some years afterward I found this passage, written by David Abram:

Naturally then, the mountains, the creatures, the entire non-human world is struggling to make contact with us. The plants we eat or smoke are trying to ask us what we are up to; the animals are signalling to us in our dreams or in forests; the whole Earth is rumbling and straining to let us remember that we are of it, that this planet, this macrocosm is our flesh, that the grasses are our hair, the trees our hands, the rivers our blood, that the Earth is our real body and that it is alive.[4]

I stayed on to finish the season and went home to Puget Sound with four thousand dollars in my pocket, more than I had ever made in an equivalent time before. I had managed—hundreds of times—to keep my feet out of the vicious coils of rope that could have pulled me into the killingly cold brine as they raced out with the net. I had also learned the ropes of the industrial hierarchy: it wasn't long before I had lobbied my way into the cook's job, which no one else wanted much anyway, so I no longer had to perform that mad dance stacking web on the stern. (During a set, the cook was the person who held the push-button box that stopped and started the power gurdy.) I had managed to not quite drink myself to death at the bars in Ketchikan and Hoonah and Petersberg during the intervals between four-day openings. At the end of the season I knew I wouldn't return; I ended my industrial fishing career muttering comparisons to the last of the buffalo hunters. From that point on I would do my killing for food one creature at a time.

I had gone west to make my fortune, like many others had before me. But I had found a great deal more than the wad of money that would keep me in the months to come. If the purse seine boat was a model of a commodity economy, salmon had shown me that it was floating in a sea of natural provision, the boundless generosity of the Earth. Salmon was but one of the more dramatic expressions of the gift of food, the gift of life. That revelation was itself a gift that would keep me forever if I could learn to translate the obligation it placed upon me. Lewis Hyde, in his priceless book *The Gift: Imagination and the Erotic Life of Property,* has this to say about that obligation: "The gift that cannot be given away ceases to be a gift. The spirit of the gift is kept alive by its constant donation." The gift that does not continue to move, dies.

In part, I have come to be by the river on this winter morning in 1983, ten years after my season on the purse seiner, in a half-conscious attempt to keep the gift moving. And, as Hyde also says, "the giving of gifts tends to establish a relationship between the parties involved." In the hour of heightened perception after the salmon eggs have been fertilized, the little group in attendance is experiencing a new range of relationships. We are bound to each other through our tentative and cautious engagement with the very processes of creation. We are related through direct engagement with a race of salmon; the fertilized eggs have been tenderly placed in the nursery built with our own hands; the blood of the mother fish is still seeping into the ground nearby. We are bound to the people, our watershed neighbors, who will tend the eggs and their emergent fry, and to the children who will return them to the wild in a few months. Most importantly, we have begun our engagement with a place, a place defined by the waters of the river we work in, a place where we may yet come to be at home.

What shall we call ourselves more than the people or human beings who live in the place where we live? What then is the name of the place where we live but our saying here or there so & so did such & such that time when he lived in the place in the gully?

JERRY MARTIEN

THROUGH the 1950s and 1960s, Mario Macchi ran a small sport-fishing service at Shelter Cove, a bight in the coast toward the southern headwaters of the Mattole drainage. The cove offered a safe anchorage against the prevailing northern winds of summer, and the serious recreational fisher could moor a boat there for a week or two at a time and fill a vacation with some excellent offshore fishing. Nat Bingham had come up from Fort Bragg, a commercial salmon port twenty miles to the south, and anchored his fully rigged salmon troller, the *Ariel,* in the cove in 1969. Nat was exploring new fishing waters along with the possibilities of a different way of life. His arrival would have the effect of setting in motion an interesting, if short-lived, local economy.

Nat and his family had erected a tepee on friends' land in Whale Gulch. According to Peter Van Arsdale, another Whale Gulch newcomer, some of the newer settlers in the area were fascinated by Nat. He personified those aspects of fishing that were likely to be attractive to those in search of a new way to live. Gone before dawn to work his boat, he could be seen in the afternoons strolling down the dirt roads of Whale Gulch, the tops of his high rubber boots rolled down, distributing his incidental catch of bottom fish to anyone who was interested. He would stop and visit and take the time to show a novice the trick of cleaning the spiny but delicious rockfish without wounding one's hands on the poisonous spines. He shared stories of the luck of the catch of the day, how the salmon were running, and how Mario was beginning to find it worthwhile to run Nat's catch up to Eureka, sixty miles to the north, to sell it.

It was not so much Nat's generosity that caught the attention of the new settlers. This was, after all, the sixties, and the serendipitous gift was one of the many unspoken articles of faith that has made that time so difficult to describe for historians who have limited themselves to a merely political context. What was different about Nat was the way he carried himself in the world. He *looked* like a fisherman. He seemed to personify a certain sane and healthy economic relationship to the larger world that was evading most of the back-to-the-landers. As he moved easily through his new milieu he radiated a mixture of intelligent contentment and focused purpose; he seemed to have an easy relationship to both the natural world and the cash-flow problem that complicated any vision of a simple life within a subsistence economy.

It was predictable that some of the new settlers would be drawn to this expression of local economy and primary production. Before long, there was a rag-tag collection of day boats anchored in Shelter Cove, known affectionately as the Mosquito Fleet. Fishing with the Mosquito Fleet was where Stevie had gained his love of salmon. Icing the daily catch and

running it up to Eureka became a larger part of Mario's operation. For a few years a seasonal living could be made by the
handful of people eccentric enough to maintain small boats
powered by inboard-outboard engines, with a little cabin for
shelter and a couple of gurdies, usually powered by a hand
crank, to run the trolling lines—not only hippies, but also
schoolteachers on summer break and loggers who were getting old enough to know that the next hernia might not heal
or who had been through one too many near-deadly acci-
dents. Get out at dawn and get back before the afternoon
winds pick up. On a good day, hook a score or more of the big
king salmon or the smaller, sleeker silvers, anchor your boat
in the cove and skiff the catch of the day into Mario's place. A
nice life until the October winds shift to the south and Shelter Cove loses its shelter and the salmon go up into the rivers.

The Mosquito Fleet prospered for a while in a modest way,
in part because the novices were enjoying themselves so
much. They were a gung-ho bunch. On the rare days when
the afternoon northerlies failed to appear, and the fishing
was good, the little fleet might not straggle back into the
cove until after dark.

By 1978, though, the fleet had dwindled to a handful of
larger boats: not enough salmon were being caught to sustain
more. (Twenty years later, research would show that ocean
conditions move through little-understood cycles which
produce peaks and troughs of productivity at thirty-year intervals. The last peak had occurred around 1960, some ten
years before the genesis of the little fishery. Without being
aware of it, the new fishers were riding a line on a graph, a
line that was plunging down more steeply than it had plunged
in the past because this turn in the cycle coincided with the
delayed effects of the unregulated logging frenzy of the previous two decades on freshwater salmon habitat.)

As an economic phenomenon, the little local fishery was ephemeral. But the experience changed the lives of some of its participants in ways that were to be enduring.

Sandy Tilles, who had fished for several years out of Shelter Cove, was among those who were attempting to reconfigure their lives once more, but she wasn't quite ready to give up on salmon yet. While the state processes of regulation were still clinging to a science that resisted relating the results of misguided land-use practices to the decline of the anadromous fisheries, common sense and casual observation of the damage that had been done to freshwater habitats was beginning to prevail among the people who lived in the watersheds—and, lately, among the people who were still fishing commercially.

Sandy had friends at the Redwoods Monastery, inhabited by women of the Cistercian order. The monastery is located within the last stand of uncut redwood and Douglas-fir forest in the river basin of the Mattole, not far from its headwaters. In 1978, the sisters, many of whom were deeply and spiritually attached to the functional ecosystem within which they performed their practice, agreed to host a meeting of concerned fisherfolk and local people. The purpose of the meeting was to discuss the decline of the Mattole salmon runs and to brainstorm about what strategies, if any, were available to the inhabitants of hurt places.

Richard Gienger was there, and he shared some of the insights gained through the streambank stabilization work he and a small crew and a horse were beginning to do on Indian Creek. Nat Bingham showed up, greeting old friends. Nat was already on the path that would become his life: he had become a member of the board of the Pacific Coast Federation of Fishermen's Associations and was beginning to spend as much time politicking as he did fishing. Just now he was thinking about spending the next winter tending a stream-side incubator in a remote reach of the Tenmile River, another coastal stream to the south.

Jerry Kreger, a forest geologist who had once worked for the U.S. Forest Service, was now homesteading up on Mattole Canyon Creek, a drainage that had been hit hard by the floods of 1955 and 1964. The creek runs through deep canyons for most of its length, with canyon slopes that loom up two hundred feet and more above its channel. The floods, following intensive logging, had destabilized whole mile-long stretches of the inner gorge and left them denuded not only of vegetation but of the soils necessary for recovery. Now, fourteen years later, the inner gorges remained raw, bleeding sediments into the creek every winter. Kreger had begun an effort to help the creek recover by collecting red alder seed cones and floating them downstream in large numbers as the water receded each winter, imitating the natural processes by which alder colonize and stabilize a shore; now he was gathering the seeds of coyote brush and whitethorn as well, these being two local brush species that require minimal soil or water to germinate, to see if their broadcast seed would sprout on the steep slopes above. Mattole Canyon Creek is large enough so that king salmon were still seeking access to it through the enormous delta of debris that had formed at its mouth, and Kreger described how he and a few neighbors used picks and shovels to cut access channels for the fish through the too-shallow water that fanned across the delta.

The meeting ended without any collective resolution, but the thirty or forty people who attended left with a host of new possibilities for direct action and practical, local approaches to a challenge they were beginning to understand as a personal and community imperative.

David Simpson was one of the few people from downstream who attended the meeting at the monastery. He had once lived near the Mattole's headwaters, but more recently he and his partner, Jane Lapiner, had bought property in the lower Mattole, near its confluence with the ocean. Later in the year, David attended a second meeting, closer to his new home.

This meeting was called by T. K. "Boss" Clark, a scion of one of the earliest white settlers, to discuss the disappearance of the salmon in the river, and was held at the Grange Hall located in the lower reaches of the river basin. (The Grange was the closest thing to either local government or a focus for the ranching community in the lower valley, with the possible exception of its little school district.)

Boss had invited the local Department of Fish and Game biologist to chair the meeting.

Many of the people in the room had benefited from the logging boom of the fifties and sixties; they had experienced it as a welcome windfall just as ranching subsidies were drying up after World War II. The very trees that war-driven government policies had encouraged them to simply destroy in order to expand meat-producing pasture had suddenly become worth something in their own right—worth a lot. It takes a lot of land to make a living from grazing animals, and these people had been paying taxes on the potential value of standing timber on thousands of acres of land surrounding their productive grasslands, timberland that produced little income because of the remoteness and difficulty of the landscape. But the technologies of World War II had spun off the highly mobile track-driven bulldozer, which could deliver the large Douglas-firs for conversion to two-by-fours for a national building boom driven by the affluence of the returning soldiers. It hadn't taken much more than a back-of-

the-envelope calculation to identify a new windfall that
might promise another generation of survival. (By 1956, the
tax had risen to $2.80 an acre, a significant burden on a local
economy that was by nature marginal. After the timber was
taken out, a one-time yield tax was to be paid, and the annual
taxes on the deforested land would be reduced to the current
assessment of land value minus timber: $.22 an acre.) To cut
had been an obvious choice, a no-brainer.

Few of the ranchers had known much about the costs and
techniques of logging, and many had been taken for a ride by
the first gyppo loggers who early on had poured into the valley to contract the work, but some of them had profited
handsomely. They didn't want to hear the biologist's rather
timid suggestion that freshwater habitat destruction was a
major factor in the diminishment of the Mattole salmon.
They could find a dozen other reasons for the decline of the
salmon runs: over-fishing at sea, the protection of nonhuman
predators, the Japanese factory ships.

A favorite target for blame was the state as represented
by the agencies charged with the management of wildlife—
"the Fish and Game," for short. The rush of environmental
protection legislation that had poured forth during 1970s,
on both state and federal levels, had amazed and insulted the
ranchers and put them in a defensive relationship to government in general. As a group, they felt violated and betrayed.
The expanded sense of the public trust implicit in the new
laws ran directly counter to a libertarianism grounded in
strongly held notions of the inviolability of private property
rights—the Jeffersonian ideology that landed farmers were
the backbone of the nation. This was a roomful of survivors
who had wrested a living out of a hard country by the trial
and error of several generations. At this point, any government representative was likely to be identified as a running
dog of the damned environmentalists.

The fisheries biologist was in a difficult position, carrying a message that no one wanted to hear to an angry crowd. While it wasn't true that the new environmental regulations were the *cause* of the decline, as some of the ranchers liked to claim, the practices of the DFG had certainly not succeeded in protecting a resource toward which the ranchers felt a strong proprietary sense.

And they did want their salmon back. The cliches of historical salmon abundance were vivid memories in the lives of the generation that this Grange gathering represented. The oldest of them had *seen* salmon running so thick you could "walk across the river on their backs." They had *been* on the backs of the horses that had been spooked so badly by the creeks full of spawning fish that they reared back and refused to ford the streams. Even thirty years before, a veritable storm of salmon would have poured into the river when its mouth opened in the fall. People with spears and gaff hooks would have been there to take as many as they could. Wagonloads of fresh salmon had been hauled out of the estuary to be home-canned or smoked for winter sustenance. When the wagons passed the home of a neighbor too old or infirm to take part in the feverish food-gathering, it had been the tradition to toss a large fish or two onto that person's porch. Abundant salmon, along with venison, had worked as a sort of natural insurance policy that carried the ranchers through rough times. No one had given much thought as to who or what was paying the premiums. Now, in the span of a generation, this rock of sustenance had been reduced to rubble, and no one was sure what hammer had broken it.

David remembers the tone of the meeting. The ranchers spoke of the good old days, when DFG had encouraged them to shoot nonhuman salmon predators—game management in the old style. The shooters would get together and walk down the river firing at any of the creatures that were competing with them: fish ducks (mergansers), river otters, and especially seals and sea lions, the predators that seemed to generate the most anger, perhaps because they were both larger and more able than any of the men. But killing the sea lions and seals that preyed on salmon at the mouth of the river had been outlawed by the Sea Mammal Protection Act of 1972. Sea lions! Protected![1]

"And what about them cranes and mud ducks?" Boss Clark roared.

The biologist gulped. "Cranes? You mean the great blue herons and snowy egrets?"

T. K. held his palms to the sky in a gesture that said, Isn't it obvious? The biologist tried to pass the buck. "Mr. Clark, you've got to understand, the wildlife biologists would say that our fish are just providing food for their birds. You . . . you . . ."—he searched for a way to say what was, to him, so self-evident—"you just can't *do* that kind of thing anymore."

"Shoot," said Boss Clark in an aside purposely loud enough for the whole room to hear. "Next thing you know, they'll be telling us we shouldn't have run the Indians outta here."

As the meeting ended the ranchers stood around grousing as the biologist hurriedly packed up his gear. David approached T. K. Clark a little diffidently. Clark was related by blood or history to a significant number of the people in the room. If anyone in the lower Mattole had a claim to being an elder, he had the strongest credentials.

"Mr. Clark," David said, "I'm not a particularly religious man, but I do believe that each species has a purpose in the scheme of things. I'm not sure we know enough to feel comfortable about just wiping them out." Boss Clark drew himself to his full height and to the full dignity of his eighty-some

years. (The Clark Ranch had been running sheep since
1922.[2] In the same year that sea lions had been protected, a
poison called 1080, used widely to kill coyotes that preyed
on sheep, had been outlawed by the Nixon administration—
more evidence from a sheep rancher's point of view that the
government was determined to wipe out the ranching tradition. The coyote population had begun to go up at about the
same time the ranchers began to see the long-haired new
people moving into the lower valley. In some minds, these
phenomena were not unrelated.) Clark's voice was modu-
lated, but powerful.

"Does that mean coyotes, too?" he asked. It was not a rhe-
torical question.

The second meeting of 1978, like the first, resulted in
no clear resolve. But for the second time, David heard about
stream-side incubators, this time from a semi-retired logger
who had seen incubator boxes used to test the toxicity of
effluents downstream of a pulp mill.

By early 1978, after seven years of the boating and
fishing life on Puget Sound, I had moved to San Francisco to
live and work with my longtime comrades Peter Berg and
Judy Goldhaft, and to fall in love with the woman who would
become my life partner, Nina Blasenheim. I was managing
the office of the fledgling Planet Drum Foundation out of Peter and Judy's basement and walking across town each evening to spend time with Nina.

Planet Drum had been established just a few years earlier
to promote, define, and serve the emerging bioregional
movement. In 1977, Peter Berg and renowned California
ecologist Raymond Dasmann had published an essay in *The
Ecologist*, "Reinhabiting California," that became one of the

defining documents of the new grassroots movement. "Bio-region" they wrote, "refers both to a geographical terrain and a terrain of consciousness—to a place and the ideas that have developed about how to live in that place. . . . There is a distinct resonance among living things and the factors which influence them that occurs within each separate place on the planet. Discovering and describing that resonance is the best way to describe a bioregion."[3]

By midyear, Nina and I had set up housekeeping together and were beginning to plan a future. She had completed a course of nurse's training and was doing an internship on the graveyard shift at San Francisco General Hospital. I was supplementing my income by working a few days a week in a carpenters' collective. My ten years of living on the edges of the wild and Nina's two years on a communal farm in rural Pennsylvania had given each of us enough experience to know that life in the city was not for us. Nina's daughter, Angeline, was a precocious nine years old and the public schools in the city were getting worse rather than better. As for me, a year of promoting and developing bioregional *ideas* had left me impatient. It was time to immerse ourselves in the waters of an actual place beyond the city and see if we (and our ideas) would sink or swim.

When Nina's father, Leo, offered her a small down payment on a piece of property of her choice, the offer coincided in the happy synchronicity of an affordable partnership in a parcel of land close to the home of our friends David and Jane and their children, near the mouth of the Mattole River. Salmon country.

We had first met David and Jane ten years earlier, when we had all been involved in the cultural ferment of the creative cauldron that was San Francisco in 1967–68. We had experienced there an intensity of mutuality and interde-

pendence that was illuminating and powerful; we thought
we were rediscovering tribalism, which we were not, but the
experience had produced many relationships that have endured.

That time had passed, but our fascination with the potential of self-actualizing community stayed with us. Our paths
diverged, but David and I stayed in touch. While I was off in
Puget Sound and Nina was in rural Pennsylvania, David and
Jane built a home on the back of a ton-and-a-half GMC truck
in which they traveled for some time as they built a family:
Gabrielle, Jane's daughter by a previous alliance; Omar,
whose mother had delivered him into David and Jane's care
when he was only weeks old; and Sierra, born a year later in
the back of the housetruck. By 1970, they had gravitated to
the headwaters of the Mattole, where they parked their
house in an encampment of new settlers near the headwaters
of the river. (The new wave of back-to-the-landers called
themselves "new settlers" as a response to the much less
neutral names some of the old-timers had for them. But
some reasoned that the present people of the Mattole were
all new settlers—there wasn't anyone living in the drainage
who could claim more than a hundred and thirty years of
family history there.)

When the large Matthews Ranch, near the mouth of the
Mattole, was subdivided in the early seventies, David and
Jane took advantage of the developer's generous financing to
buy a place of their own, a windswept hilltop with little
water but a magnificent view of the river and the ocean.

While my interests were turning in the direction of
salmon as a phenomenon that informed the consciousness of
the whole Pacific Rim, David was increasingly drawn to the
specificity of the race of fish that informed and fed his neighbors in the valley that spread out below his new home.

Both Nina and I had visited David and Jane independently

during their sojourn in the Mattole. Once they had their own place, we visited more often, and together. The setting had a salubrious and consistent effect on us; the physical ambience generated a euphoria which remained constant as long as we were there and which was reliably available whenever we returned—a euphoria I came to recognize as rising out of the place itself.

In the summer of 1978, sometime between the two meetings that David attended, Nina and Angeline and I drove up to spend a few weeks working on the half-finished barn we had chosen to make our home.

That year David and I and a few others also began to talk regularly about Mattole salmon, and between us we tracked down a technical paper about experiments with stream-side incubation in Alaska and Washington. The ideas and the technology seemed to lend themselves to the conditions of Mattole salmon as well as to our predispositions for localized social activism. For myself, the plans that began to emerge also served another purpose: they would allow me to immerse myself once more in the world of salmon in a way that didn't make me feel ambivalent.

Our irregular conversations produced enough understanding of the freshwater requirements of the native fish to be able to isolate two conditions that were limiting their reproductive success: spawning gravels had been jammed with sediment to the degree that too few eggs were surviving their period of incubation, and the few fingerlings that did emerge found a river with too few deep pools and too little stream-side shade to provide them with an adequately cool rearing habitat during the time they spent growing in the river, before they migrated to sea. We reasoned that if we could capture native eggs, fertilize them, and incubate them in small structures that imitated the gravels in an optimally functioning river, we would be treating the first of these limitations, a scarcity of good spawning habitat.

Naively, we imagined that we could make a difference within two or three king salmon life cycles—six to ten years, say. More cannily, we knew that there was enough interest among local people of every persuasion that we could locate stream-side incubators in the yards of volunteers. Backyard passion would supply the level of volunteerism needed for the daily maintenance of the little household hatcheries we envisioned. The structures we imagined had no moving parts; they would take their water from gravity flow systems that would require no pumps or generators but only that their filters be cleaned often, especially during winter storms. Everyone who lived in the hills already knew how to install and maintain such systems; their household water supplies depended on them. We knew skilled carpenters who could build the incubators (which we were already calling hatchboxes), welders who could knock up adequate filters out of discarded fifty-gallon metal drums. Rural people have plenty of experience in scrounging building materials.

A vision of a new relationship between salmon and settler bloomed in our imaginations like algae in a warm pond. We contacted a rural sport-fishing group in Oklahoma that was experimenting with hatching trout in Vibert boxes, little plastic mesh containers filled with fertilized eggs and buried in stream bottoms. Our long-distance telephone call was answered in an enthusiastic Okie twang: "Never saw nothing like it! It's just like raising chickens. You nurse those eggs and people just love those little critters, just like they was their own chickens!" Yes. It may have been personally difficult to imagine falling in love with chickens, but collectively we were able to imagine our hatchboxes proliferating under the tender care of residents on every creek with the result that folks would fall in love with their local salmon runs, learn to run their homesteads and ranches in ways that would do the fish no harm, defend their watersheds against industrial forces from outside with a newfound passion.

If we weren't yet sure of the details of how to capture and breed wild fish, those were skills we could learn. Someone had a copy of Alfred Kroeber's encyclopedic paper on indigenous methods of trapping fish in northwest California: we would start from there. We all knew how to catch fish for food, didn't we? Surely capturing fish in the service of their inborn biological imperative couldn't be so difficult.

There was, of course, the problem of the state. Much of our collective experience with the state had to do with evading it. We ran trucks with broken taillights; we built homes without consulting building inspectors; on one or two occasions some of us may even have hunted or fished without the appropriate license. Ranch and farm trucks that never left the valley often ran for decades without updated plates, owner registrations, inspection stickers. Some of the new settlers in particular hadn't filed an income tax form for years. It was attractive, even thrilling, to think about mounting our effort as a guerrilla operation. Why not? There was just enough of the spirit of the sixties left among the Mattole valley newcomers to make attractive the idea of free people working in the service of the wild—perhaps to revive some fading dreams of a functional social anarchism.

The discussion was short-lived. The argument prevailed that if our restoration strategy had as much potential as we thought it did, we would certainly want the fruit of our experiments and experiences to be available not only to all people in the Mattole but to people in other watersheds. And we most certainly would need the advice of a whole range of experts, few of whom shared a romance with living beyond the law.

The first step, then, was to obtain the blessing of the California Department of Fish and Game. The DFG had a carefully delineated set of regulations regarding the taking of salmon from rivers. The rules laid out gear restrictions, bag limits, and geographical constraints designed to keep recreational fishers off the spawning grounds. Over time, we would ask to be allowed to violate each and every one of those restrictions. We knew that our initiative would be met with resistance; we were, directly and indirectly, challenging a whole set of assumptions that lay behind the history of state regulation of resources.

The obstacles to our notions began to identify themselves in the first series of phone calls to Sacramento. We reached Bob Rawstron, head of the Inland Fisheries Division of DFG, a crusty, straight-talking veteran who had come up through the ranks of field biologists to head the division that concerned itself with anadromous fisheries. The Department of Fish and Game was a poor cousin in the family of resources agencies in California, a state very wealthy in resources. It wasn't that various governors and legislatures hadn't realized the value of California's fisheries and game animals—as translated into tourist dollars, deer tags, fishing licenses, and so on—it was just that other resources were so much *more* valuable. After the water and agriculture and timber agencies had taken their slice of the annual budget, the DFG got what was left. The Department of Fish and Game dealt with its short-handedness through a sort of riverine triage based on production numbers. Department monies went to places that would produce the most obvious results. It was

in early conversations with the DFG that we first heard a bureaucratic catch-phrase we would come to loathe: "more
bang for the buck."

Rawstron himself was bluff and straightforward. The
Mattole, he told us, had no future as a salmon producer. Fish
and Game had written it off as damaged beyond repair. And
even when it had been in good shape (he asked us to realize),
its tens of thousands of salmon faded to insignificance when
compared to the millions pumped out of the hatcheries on
the Sacramento and the Klamath. Yes, he knew we were
offering our services as volunteers (he tried hard to hide his
impatience), but did we realize how much department time
would be required to provide expert supervision for our misplaced do-gooder ambitions? He didn't actually say "misplaced" or "do-gooder," but as our insistent conversations
took up more and more of his time, the busy man had difficulty keeping the sarcasm out of his voice. He was after all, a
lifetime professional dealing with amateurs who seemed to
have a hard time understanding the meaning of no.

A day spent in the Eureka office of the DFG to collect historical information about Mattole salmon populations
showed us that Rawstron was by no means the author of the
policy that gave short shrift to small rivers. A day of sorting
and copying had produced no more than a very thin file
folder of information on the Mattole. Much of the monitoring data recorded there revealed fieldwork limited to stopping the state vehicle for a few moments and rolling down
the window to take a look. This is understandable from a
purely practical point of view; then, as now, two state biologists covered a two-county area approximately the size of the
state of Delaware. It took most of a day simply to drive from
the Eureka office, traverse the length of the river and return
home. To actually get out of the truck and count fish in such

an insignificant river could only be done at the expense of
time that might be spent on larger, more productive waterways.

The bright side of the picture was that the Mattole had also
been spared the attention of the hatchery programs that had
been the showboat centerpiece of state fisheries management
for a century.

Right alongside our ambition to save our local native gene
pool was the ambition to test the proposition that technologies are benign tools guided to one consequence or another
by the ethic that is applied to their use. We would be attempting to demystify hatchery science and then to turn it
on its head—to use it as a way of putting ourselves in the position of learning from the salmon rather than as a way to re-
organize nature.

We knew enough by now to understand that centralized
hatcheries were a mechanical approach to maintaining
salmon that had little resemblance to the way that salmon
manage themselves. And we knew one other thing, which
anyone who depends on machines knows—we knew that
machines break. We knew about Murphy's Law. We knew
firsthand about the consistency of human error. We also
knew enough to know that the wild salmon native to our
river would decline into extinction without some action on
our part.

As an adjective, the word *wild* is used so indiscriminately
as to muddle our thinking. Wild youth. Wild hair. Wild
beast. But if the word is fastidiously defined to describe a ho-
meostatic, self-organized relationship that does not require
management from outside itself, then it can provide us with
a meditation large enough to occupy a lifetime. By this definition our breath is wild. Our heartbeat is wild. Our diges-
tive systems are wild, made up as they are of multiple organ-

isms largely defined by their mutual function. Any cubic foot of healthy soil is a relational cell of the wild of such complexity as to defy rational analysis. By engaging the health of another species, by engaging salmon as an expression of our own survival, could we turn ourselves and our neighbors in the direction of a wilder, self-organizing relationship to each other and to the world close at hand?

The interest of the state assumed central importance in comparison to the individual parts. The whole was greater than the sum of its parts ... the common interest or happiness of the state could be different from the interest and happinesses of the individual members or their sum.

CAROLYN MERCHANT, *The Death of Nature*

OR A LITTLE while, so the plan went, Nina and I would remain in San Francisco to make money to support our move to the Mattole. But we made another trip north in the early summer of 1979 to do some more work on our future home.

I was in a hurry to get the south end of the barn sided, so I didn't take the time to build a scaffolding. I was using a wooden extension ladder splattered with twenty years of paint it had accumulated before its original owner had switched to a lighter aluminum rig and sold the old one to me for twenty-five dollars. The wall was only thirty feet long, I told myself, ignoring the fact that under the roof beam it was also thirty feet high. I was nailing up full-dimensional one-by-ten fir planks on a vertical run. Every other plank, I would move the ladder and shim up one leg of it to compensate for the slope of the ground. I was congratulating myself that it was taking me only a little over two days to wrestle the heavy thirty-foot planks into place and nail them up; building and taking down a scaffolding would have eaten up another full day. I had begun at the top of the slope, and when I got to the last board I was as high above the ground as the job would take me. I couldn't move the ladder again without it getting in the way of the job, so I just leaned out a little farther to sink the first nail into the last plank . . .

I don't remember falling, but I must have gone down head-first and put out my arms to break the fall: both wrists were shattered and required stainless steel pins at elbow and wrist; casts on both arms extended from knuckles to well above the elbows. After nine weeks the casts were removed and I walked around for two days with my arms clutched to my chest, feeling naked and vulnerable in a way that is usually available only in dreams.

Nina and her daughter Angeline and I now had a new time-table. The doctors were saying I'd need a year of physical therapy before I'd be pounding any more nails. After failing the street-map test twice, I got a job driving for Yellow Cab back in San Francisco. For a year of ten-hour nights I became a corpuscle in the streets that are the bloodstreams of modern cities. Given power steering, it was a job with physical therapy built in. And as I got better at the job, the bloodstream seemed too sluggish a metaphor for my function in the city. I began to feel, rather, like a neuron in the quick and ever-wakeful brain of the metropolis. The city was thinking its own big thoughts that were beyond my comprehension; my passengers were messages and it was my job to carry them, on demand, from one urban ganglion to another.

The friendlier passengers would ask me about my life. I was just driving until my wrists got strong, I told them, and until I piled up enough money to move to a remote place in northern California and save the salmon there. I noticed that the story improved tips. The customers either thought I was slightly deranged and could use the extra help, or they thought I was a good-hearted innocent and the story brought out the protective parent in them.

David and I continued to strategize by telephone. He continued to seek out whatever could be learned about Mattole salmon, drummed up enthusiasm for a community effort, and did what he could to educate the local poachers. Since the latter was a euphemism for walking the banks of the lower river at night and putting oneself between the fish and the fishermen, I was just as happy it was him doing it rather than me. Meanwhile, I was only an hour's ride from Sacramento, the home of one of the first bureaucratic hurdles to be crossed if our ideas were going to take us into the river.

Bob Rawstron had delegated our inability to take no for an answer to other people in the Anadromous Branch of the Inland Fishery Division of the DFG, functionaries who concerned themselves with hatchery administration. The DFG's Steve Taylor and Jack Robinson were at least willing to devote more time to our ideas, to discuss their implications and the problems and risks that came along with them in some detail. The meetings were held at Rancho Cordova, the site of the DFG's most productive salmon hatchery on the Sacramento River, just upstream of the capital. Taylor and Robinson were professionals; they had a good deal of education invested in their careers along with a couple of decades of tolerating bureaucratic jostling and tedium. They couldn't quite conceive that nonprofessionals, people off the street so to speak, could assume any aspect of the trust and dedication their life histories represented. Most of the work we were describing, though, was menial, commonly handled by seasonal aides who were usually students, or by civil servants at the very bottom of the institutional ladder: cleaning filters, installing temporary structures, performing rudimentary surveys. These jobs, Robinson and Taylor came to concede, could be handled by locals as long as they were carefully supervised by Department of Fish and Game personnel. When it came to taking eggs and fertilizing them, however, we were getting into an area so arcane, the men intimated, that it was unlikely that we would be able to learn to do it.

We knew better, but kept our peace. The major stumbling block we would somehow need to overcome was to convince the DFG to give certain civilians, under the auspices of a nonprofit organization, fishing privileges not allowed to anyone else in the state. In order to improve the survival of *native* stocks, we would have to set traps or nets in the rivers, a practice strictly forbidden to either commercial or recreational fishers. We were asking that regulations designed to be rigid and uncompromising become suddenly flexible enough to accommodate local responses to local conditions. It was unprecedented.

As it became apparent that we were discussing decisions that could only be made at a higher level of administration, an audience was arranged with Charles Fullerton, director of the California Department of Fish and Game—the man at the top. Fullerton was a manager in the old style, a politically savvy survivor of several very different administrations. I arrived for the appointment alone. Although I wore a necktie, when I checked in the mirror I could see someone who still looked like he drove taxi for a living.

After allowing me to wait in a receptionist's office for half an hour, Director Fullerton received me behind a firmly latched door. He sat on the far side of an office that was as large as the apartment I shared with Nina and Angeline. Fullerton was a bulky man who didn't seem fat. He had mastered the art of grooming so completely that from the doorway he seemed to glow like a golden statue of the Buddha. I have read that commercial fishing is the most dangerous job in America, with a mortality rate of 104 deaths for every 100,000 people employed. (Taxi drivers rank fifth, after loggers and pilots.) As I walked across the room toward the single straight chair on the victim's side of the huge desk that was the dominant piece of furniture in the room, I had time to wonder why I felt smaller and more vulnerable now than I ever had on the deck of a small fishing boat in choppy seas.

I have little memory of what the director said in the five minutes we spent together, but I left his office with the knowledge that while he admired the fervor and spirit of our proposal, I had to understand that budgets were established and appropriated far in advance, that policy changes sometimes took years of deliberation, that he would certainly take our proposal under advisement, and thanks very much for traveling all this way.

Our governing bodies in the United States continue to convince us that they are firmly founded on the principles of life, liberty, and the pursuit of happiness. But there is a happiness of the state that grows larger than the well-being of individuals guaranteed by the Constitution. The overriding priority of the happiness of the state is that its institutions maintain their inviolability. Fullerton's long tenure demonstrated as well as anything that he was a good servant of the happiness of the state.

There are times when my most cherished perceptions grow hollow and translucent and lie strewn in the mind like the transparent skeletons of jellyfish on a deserted beach. My interview with Director Fullerton seriously diminished my

confidence. As the elevator carried me down from the four-
teenth floor of the Natural Resources Building, leaving my
stomach behind, I realized that the same minds that had built
this tower had built the Shasta Dam, which had eliminated a
third of the spawning habitat for the salmon of the Sacramento drainage, had built the Friant Dam and the Delta-
Mendota Canal, which had effectively killed the great San
Joaquin River runs by dewatering the river. The great inland
valley that contained this skyscraper through which I was
falling had been transformed in a scant century by a gargan-
tuan human effort to contain a river intent on turning the
lower half of its valley into swamplands—places of incredible fertility, natural nurseries and pantries for a myriad of
creatures—for half of every year. But swamps did not fit into
an economic interpretation of the landscape; there had been
few arguments against the rationality of "reclaiming" the
wetlands for farming.

The attempt to contain the river was begun by farmers
building dikes with shovels and wheelbarrows, but then the
work of local farmers was subsumed by the largest hydraulic
management initiative on the planet, the Central Valley
Project. Local struggles were displaced by centralized planning and professional engineering expertise, by the U.S.
Army Corps of Engineers and the federal Bureau of Recla-
mation. Today the swamps are mostly gone, and the farm-
lands are protected from flood consistently enough so that
agribusiness can use the Central Valley to feed a large part of
the planet's human population. But the soils are becoming
saline and the water table is sinking. The salmon that remain
in the rivers are dependent on a frail technology. "One-
hundred-year" floods become more frequent, as do ruptures
in emergency-fund accounts to repair the damages done by
them. There are few people left living who can remember

the previous configurations of the valley, its richness of provision, its diversity of habitat. After ten thousand years of a
different set of relationships between people and place, the
reconstructed landscape with its purely economic rationale
had become the only context in which human social organization could imagine itself.

But at the peripheries of the reconstructed landscape,
there are places that still maintain some of their original
power to shape and direct the minds of their inhabitants. The
Mattole basin has its own set of geological and hydrological
determinants on a scale so grand as to keep their control outside the capabilities of even the most ambitious engineer.
The fact that the Mattole basin is not only the wettest place
in California, but also the most tectonically active single area
in continental North America had frustrated the plans of
the state road builders and had probably contributed to the
fact that dam-building engineers hadn't wandered into the
Mattole until their employment opportunities in California
were nearly used up. (When they did, in the early 1970s,
people living in the drainage had unified in opposition and
beaten back proposals for a "flood control" dam.)

Yet even in the Mattole, the wild systems that offer an alternative way of thinking had been diminished to a point
nearing invisibility. More than 90 percent of the ancient forests of the Mattole were gone. Ranchers were finding it more
difficult to break even in a marketplace grown international.
The options for a human community based on the natural
provision of the place were being diminished with a rapidity
that created a sense of inevitability. The remnant native
salmon runs might very well be the fulcrum on which the integrity of the place teetered.

By the time I reached the street floor, I had reconvinced
myself that an effort to engage people with the evolutionary

and geological processes of their collective home would surely be an effort in service of their own self-interest and their pursuit of happiness. My convictions gained weight as the elevator plunged. The happiness of people has a great deal in common with the happiness of salmon. And the happiness of salmon is imbedded in the ability of watersheds to provide them with what they need.

The elevator stopped at street level and my stomach caught up with me, along with a sense of mission and an inchoate faith in the power of places to teach us how to act.

Which still left the problem of where to go next. Another telephone conversation with David, in which we remembered a hole card yet to be played. Our mutual friend from our days on the streets of San Francisco, Peter Coyote, had recently been appointed as chair of the California Arts Council. Would Peter arrange an appointment with Huey Johnson, Governor Jerry Brown's cabinet-level Secretary for Resources? He would.

Huey Johnson, Fullerton's temporary boss, had an entirely different interviewing style, equally intimidating, but arranged so that situations could emerge that might have the power to surprise. Johnson had founded the Trust for Public Land, which under his direction had quickly grown into one of the most effective conservation organizations in the country. Johnson was actively engaged in the concept of sustainability a good twenty years before it became a buzzword. He was committed to finding ways to introduce into public policy some of the notions inherent in twentieth-century developments in ecology. A hugely energetic man, he was working from the conviction that the future of California depended on the maintenance of the natural processes within its boundaries. He knew his tenure in the job would be short, and he was determined to make a difference in that time. Under his guidance, the Z'berg-Nejedly Act of 1973 had been fleshed out to become the California Forest Practice Rules, which for the first time recognized that the state's forests had other functions that sometimes overrode their ability to produce timber. He was in the process of establishing the Renewable Resources Investment Fund, which would dedicate state oil revenues to the purpose of protecting and enhancing biodiversity.

Johnson's office was in the same building as Fullerton's, but it was of another culture. Amid a jumbled but handsome clutter of California native artifacts and art, in the very center of the room, a huge throne-like Tongan chair woven of bamboo hung suspended by a chain. It was in this seat that the visitor was invited to sit. The chair swung freely as I hiked myself up into it clumsily, for there was no way to do it gracefully; once I was settled my feet didn't quite touch the floor and the chair rotated slowly, first one way and then another. The visitor who had an ax to grind was hard put to remain aggressive from such a perch. My response to the discomfiting situation, to the best of my memory, was to babble. Again, I have little memory of what was said. But the meeting lasted somewhat longer than my meeting with Fullerton. Something in my disorganized presentation must have captured Huey's imagination, because by the time I had jumped down from the Tongan throne he had said that he would instruct the Department of Fish and Game to cooperate with us. He also suggested that we work with the Cooperative Fisheries Research Unit, based at Humboldt State University and funded by the U.S. Department of Fish and Wildlife.

 Dr. Roger Barnhart, the director of the Cooperative Fisheries Research Unit, introduced David and me to one of his graduate students, Gary Peterson. Gary was doing his master's thesis on the use of the Vibert box, the same device our friends in Oklahoma were using. Theoretically, this simple technology combines the efficiency of hatchery production with some of the benefits of natural processes, and its use promotes a higher survival rate of healthier fish. Gary's research was designed to determine if this claim was true. The project was close to completion when we met him, and he was bored. He had a deeply felt need, I think, to get into a creek or river and demonstrate to himself that his science was related to something alive.

The California Fisheries Restoration Foundation had been one of the recipients of our proposal for a pilot project, and it had granted us $750 for research and design, contingent on permission from the state to take native egg stock. As we closed in on permission, we accepted the grant and told Gary he could have the whole of that grand sum if he would do the science the state had failed to do and now was requiring of us. Gary would survey tributary streams, looking for rearing habitat that was "understocked" or that had supported salmon runs in the past that were now depleted. He would research the literature and deliver detailed designs for traps and weirs, primary incubation, and stream-side incubation structures. Most importantly, he would frame our arguments in the language of fisheries science, a jargon in which many of us would become fluent but of which we were mostly innocent back then.

A flurry of meetings and long distance calls ensued, in Willits, in Ukiah, in Arcata and Eureka. We interpreted Secretary Johnson's letter as instructions to the DFG to proceed with an enthusiasm that matched our own; DFG administrators seemed to read it as advising very cautious adjustments in our direction. We weren't to take fish from off their natural spawning grounds, an instruction based on admirable caution against our interfering with natural processes. But because so little was known about where salmon did spawn in the Mattole, we were limited to the lower five miles of the river, an area where winter flows swelled quickly toward flood proportions after normal rainfall. Moreover, since the eggs of females ripen toward fecundity as they proceed upstream, females were more likely to be "green" at capture and to need to be held until their eggs ripened.

Very well, Gary would lead a reconnaissance of nearby farm and homestead ponds that might serve to hold adult fish until they were ready to be spawned, an exercise we were able to turn into a workshop for interested residents. When we were informed that we would be expected to reimburse the Fish and Game biologists who were to supervise us and, further, that whenever we moved fish a biologist had to drive the truck, we began to regret our decision not to undertake the project as outlaws. But it was too late for that, and we nodded our heads in solemn agreement without a clue as to where the money might come from.

Nina and I hired a U-Haul truck and made our final move from San Francisco to Petrolia in early summer of 1980. This time I built a scaffolding to side the east wall of the barn. Then I joined in the flurry of activity that launched the effort to rescue the salmon of the Mattole.

David had been introduced by a friend, rancher John Chambers, to an executive of Pacific Lumber Company, the largest commercial landowner in the watershed. The company donated redwood for the hatchboxes that were being built by Peter Van Arsdale, Andrea Cohen, and John Vargo. Peter built a little window into his hatchbox, with a clever sliding cover, so that eggs could be observed developing without over-exposing them to sunlight. With great enthusiasm, another neighbor, Jim Groeling, one of the most highly respected craftsman-builders in the region, had taken on the job of designing and building a trap for adult fish. Groeling's home, an old working barn remodeled into a graceful home with Craftsman-style features, overlooked the river where the trap and weir would be located that first year.

Our workspace was in the cluttered yard of Rex and Ruth Rathbun's home. Perhaps cluttered is the wrong word. Someone had once told me that anyone with a neat yard must be living an ecologically unsound life—meaning what did the owner of the showplace yard do with all the stuff that might be useful some day? Rex had converted an outbuilding to a shop packed from floor to ceiling with scavenged cables and winches, bolts and nuts, and fasteners of every description. The Rathbun toolshed was always our first stop on the shopping trips set off by Gary's two- and three-page lists of building materials needed for completion of our installations.

David fretted over every detail of the rapidly growing project. He seemed to be everywhere at once, seemed to have more stamina than the rest of us. A trip with David to the post office five miles away was likely to take two hours. We never passed a truck coming toward us but that we stopped to exchange news and pleasantries, driver's-side windows rolled down, the conversations invariably lasting until another truck pulled up behind one or another of the vehicles that were blocking the road. David never had fewer than several projects going at once, and the trip to the post office might include a stop to fill the back of the truck with hay for his horses, and another to search for a part needed for another truck being repaired, or to look at a new supply of salvaged building materials hauled into the valley by a neighbor. Each of the errands and meetings in passing included some exchange of information about the state of the salmon and on the progress of the new project, some solicitation of advice or request for help. They became, in fact, the irregular meetings of the Mattole Watershed Salmon Support Group.

Gary spent most of his time that summer surveying tributary creeks, evaluating them for spawning and rearing habitat, and looking for over-summering juvenile silver salmon and steelhead, and for water sources for our planned installations. He met with Dave Miller, a fisheries biologist working for Simpson Timber, who had also become interested in hatchbox technology and had developed a design that was adapted to northern California conditions. Gary modified the design further to accommodate our need to build remote systems in places with no electricity for pumps or other devices. These designs turned into parts lists as we scrambled to build several prototypes, and into architectural drawings for inclusion in the fifty-page rationale Gary was preparing for the state. Weekdays in the valley, he slept in his van, or in David and Jane's old housetruck, or in John Vargo's cabin on our place while John was away engaged in an extended courtship. Most weekends, Gary would return to Arcata and pound away at a borrowed IBM Selectric typewriter.

There were volunteers aplenty, as there usually are at the beginning of a community effort, and Gary was willing to live on little while he provided us with professional credibility. Rex's collection of materials was rich, but it wasn't adequate to the demands we put on it. We needed literally miles of plastic pipe to deliver gravity-fed water to our incubators, along with hundreds of connectors and stainless steel hose clamps. The cheapest valves cost five dollars apiece. To augment our scavenging skills, we needed more cash than the donation jar at the local store was bringing in.

Paul Hawken, who would later devote his life to teaching corporations the advantages of environmentally inclusive accounting, had recently purchased an interest in a ranch across the river from us. Paul had been an active player in Governor Jerry Brown's campaigns and had served off and on in an advisory role to the governor's office. He had made strong connections among people who were both fiscally comfortable and predisposed to support an effort like ours. Paul wrote a form letter on a quickly improvised letterhead, and within two months had raised $4,500 for the project. Along with a few small local donations, that was the extent of our budget as we launched the Mattole hatchbox project in 1980.

September and October can be the most beautiful time of year on the California coast near Cape Mendocino. The trajectory of the sun sinks toward the southern horizon and the light softens so that it increases the depth of vision. Light seems to gain body so that the skin receives it as a warm caress. Occasional showers can relieve the crispness of the fire season and lay down the dust on the roads. The smell of moisture is erotic after four or five months of building dryness.

In the fall of the year that Nina and I finally moved to the Mattole for good, I was too wound up in particulars to appreciate the season. Once a real winter storm or two had worked its way off the Pacific, the lagoon at the mouth of the river would fill and the berm that had kept it separated from the ocean all summer would open. One thing on which all local observers agreed was that when the berm broke, king salmon were always waiting to come through into fresh water. It seemed important to be ready to capture fish at the beginning of the run, before the winter floods made our success even more unpredictable. A journal I kept recalls part of the story.

31 October 1980. What a flood of details! Should the egg trays sit up off the bottom of the incubation trough? What size and how many bolts will make the trap strong enough to withstand the force of the river but allow for quick dismantling once we want to get it out? What size pipe will allow fifteen gallons per minute to flow through the incubation boxes? And where is our next money coming from? My mind is always in two or three places at once and I make mistakes because of it.

8 November 1980. Close to midnight, a 6.5 foot high tide with westerly winds behind it. . . . At 2:35 AM we experienced the largest earthquake in recent history, 7.1 on the Richter scale with its epicenter 40 miles northwest out to sea. Our house rocked like a small boat broached to the swell. No damage but to the psyche of the girls who are here for a slumber party to celebrate Angeline's tenth birthday. They had quieted down only an hour before the house got slammed. Then it got very quiet and after what seemed a long time, a small, scared voice bleated out a question, "Ma?"

Sometime before dawn the river bar opened at its extreme northern end. . . . If there aren't salmon in the river now, there will be at the next high tide. I'm feeling small and tired this evening, a bit actor in a very large drama.

All day the river remained too high to work in and too muddy to see if the fish were moving.

10 November 1980. No rain for two days, and the level of the river has fallen. Last night we went down to greet the fish. . . . Around a fire with a willow break between us and the river, we sat and dreamed, several adults and half a dozen pre-teen kids. It was cold and very still; the only sounds came from the current of the river and the crackling of Douglas-fir limbs in the fire. When people spoke, they whispered. The first sign of salmon, a series of sounds like ripe pears being dropped into the river one by one, made everyone catch their breath at once.

All sense of purpose had left me. After all these months of preparing to capture salmon, it was enough to simply see them. . . .

Six or eight fish move slowly and languidly, breaking water but never jumping. They explore the weir without frenzy, moving along the fence methodically, searching for a way upstream. Each fish edges its way along the weir toward the stronger current and, reaching the mouth of the trap, swims right past it and retreats to hang in the current downstream. Some fish repeat this movement several times.

In order to learn more about the run, and to observe the trap, we have decided to maintain all-night watches, in shifts. Although enthralled, most of us had wandered off by midnight, the kids asleep and wrapped in blankets in our arms. John Vargo took over the watch, and at about three o'clock in the morning, he decided to take a more active approach. Poised on a plank stretched between the trap and the shore, he dip-netted two jack salmon and transferred them to the trap. Toward dawn, Greg Smith, a rancher from across the river, came down to relieve John. Together, Greg holding onto John's belt while John plunged the dip net, they captured a beautiful female king salmon which must weigh more than twenty pounds.

All knowledge is local. All knowledge is partial.

URSULA K. LE GUIN, *Four Ways to Forgiveness*

MORNING IS a container too small for the rush of spring light pouring through new foliage, tinting with a hundred shades of green the lush growth along the banks of Thompson Creek. It has been an extreme winter, an El Niño winter. The extraordinary amount of rainfall can be experienced once more in the exuberant foliage, the extra-large flower blossoms, and the creek running high and clear today, in mid-April of 1982. This creek is the longest of a series of parallel liquid ribs that join the spine of the Mattole from either side. At its confluence with the river is the monastery where watershed residents and fishermen met nearly five years earlier.

A half dozen adults carrying five-gallon buckets are led up a trail parallel to the water by a teenage guide who has grown up playing on the creek. The young man darts ahead of us. He knows the creek like an urban kid might know the tiny irregularities in the neighborhood basketball court. The buckets are heavy; they are half full of water and they slosh at each step. Lids cover the containers to prevent the loss of any of the baby fish swimming in the clear, cold water that was collected from high up in the stream. A different spot is chosen for the release of the fish from each bucket. We are challenged to see the creek through the eyes of infantile salmon as we look for nurturing habitat. We look for pools dappled with shade, knotty root systems hanging in the water, places where large trees have fallen into the creek. Marco, our guide, leads us unerringly to such places.

A ceremony has declared itself and seized our minds. The event has a completeness about it that doesn't yield easily to individualized expression. There is very little talking. My self-perception extends beyond the skin and into the air and water surrounding, taking in humans and other beings who happen to be in the nearby places. It feels as if we are being watched in return, by whom or what I couldn't say. When it comes my turn to release fish into the stream I remain squatting for a few moments to watch the progress of the miniature salmon. At first the little swimmers dart every which way, like the explosion of a fireworks display. But within seconds they have formed themselves into a small, tight school and together they seek shelter. Now the individual fish move as if from a single impulse; the water between them is like the spaces between electrons, between planets. Some force or knowledge or signal moves between the fish, as powerful and as invisible as gravity itself, to organize the swimmers into a mutual intelligence.

It makes me unreasonably happy to see this behavior. I try to imagine a similar mutuality between humans and the medium in which we move. As if to temper my giddiness, a year-old steelhead glides out from its shelter under a nearby tree root. At six or seven inches long, the year-old steelhead is of an order of magnitude larger than the juvenile king salmon, most of which are no longer than my little finger. The steelhead is a battleship among canoes. Its movements seem grand and leisurely and inevitable next to the nervous tics of the new school of fingerlings as they dart this way and that to avoid the predator. Almost too quickly to comprehend, the larger fish has swallowed one of the smaller ones whole. Even more quickly, the constellation of juvenile salmon disappears as one into the darkness beneath an overhanging bank.

During the two-plus years between its first attempts to trap king salmon and the release of successfully reared juvenile fish, the Salmon Group has learned by trial and error most of the technical expertise that will carry it on through the next twenty years of steady dedication to the survival of the native stock. The hatchbox strategy was consistently successful in that it improved the survival rate of the salmon eggs it incubated by eight to ten times over the rate that could be expected in the habitat available in a damaged river. But if salmon population numbers were the only criterion for success, the effort would only mimic the successes of industrial hatcheries in creating a product at the expense of genetic diversity.[1]

The true challenge, then, was to restore the ability of the Mattole River system to maintain its wildly productive dynamic equilibrium and so eliminate the need for a bunch of clumsy humans to intervene in another species' reproductive strategies. The effort had to grow beyond population enhancement to engagement with the healing processes of the watershed so that this place could become once again a habitat that supported the needs of all its species, including humans.

By the early 1980s, several strands of community commitment in this direction combined to make such a goal seem practical. A survey of available salmonid habitat conducted by Coastal Headwaters, an upstream community-based group, created a basis for beginning to think about the watershed as a whole. The survey also made a start at documenting the whereabouts of specific human-created obstacles to successful salmon reproduction: the logjams that prevented the upstream migration of adult fish, streambank erosion accelerated by the placement and/or poor maintenance of roads, great stretches of cooling stream-side vegetation ripped out by floodwaters that had no place else to go because the deeper channels had been filled with rubble.

More importantly, the survey required the recruitment of a cadre of area residents, who discovered among themselves a pool of expertise and the understanding necessary to experience the place as a complex knot of physical and biological and socioeconomic processes. The best naturalists, after all, usually live close by the places they observe. And the newer settlers included people trained in geology and biology who had thrown over institutional jobs that they found too full of moral contradictions. If training was needed which was not available through neighbors, field scientists from Redwood National Park or the Bureau of Land Management proved eager to share their experience once they realized how committed and highly motivated these residents were.

The state gradually reduced its restrictions on where the Salmon Group could take fish, and the group's efforts became more effective. Largely due to the lobbying of commercial fishermen, two northern California legislators were able to establish a small fund for habitat rehabilitation on salmon streams in California. Later this fund was maintained and enlarged through the willingness of commercial fishers to impose a yield tax on themselves.

Small contracts for habitat rehabilitation work became available, which allowed even more people to get an on-the-job education in the biological and geological processes of their larger home. These projects were always underfunded and inevitably required as much volunteer work as paid time to get them finished, but the woods were full of people who were delighted to be paid for one of every two or three hours they spent working in the creeks—the creeks were where they wanted to be anyway.

But these several efforts were not enough to overcome what was still a scattershot approach to watershed rehabilitation. On April Fool's Day of 1983, the workers learned just how much they didn't know—and how much of it lay beyond their best intentions—when 375 acres slid all at once right into the mainstream of the Mattole, carrying 430,000 cubic yards of soil and rubble and woody debris, enough to dam the river completely for a day. Several houses were also tumbled downhill, leaving their owners homeless. It was only the second-largest landslide in California that year, but it certainly focused people's attention on the magnitude of the problems they were engaging.

Much of the environmental damage being treated by local people through projects designed to prevent streambank erosion was the result of chronic or delayed effects of the timber boom of the fifties and sixties, a time, as we've seen, of little forest practice regulation. The thousands of miles of former skid roads that crisscrossed the drainages had become all but invisible after two decades of vegetative resurgence, but some of them continued to concentrate and divert water onto unstable slopes. The large logs that supported thousands of stream crossings had rotted in the intervening twenty years, and the torrents of El Niño came just at the time when they were ready to blow.

Past mistakes were not all that needed to be corrected, however. Industrial timberland owners were still filing harvest plans at a reduced but steady rate, often on steep and unstable slopes that had been skipped over when more accessible timber had been available. And many of the salmon workers themselves were hill-dwellers who relished their remoteness and privacy, and figured that the rutted roads full of potholes that they had inherited when logged-over ranches were subdivided were part of the cost of their way of life. The corporate forest landowners who still controlled 12 percent of the watershed land base may have been ready to continue to do damage with mechanized shovels, but all too few of the area's inhabitants had ever taken up a shovel themselves to maintain their own roads through the wet season. It became increasingly difficult to single out loggers as the sole perpetrators of crimes against the landscape.

Meanwhile, as the original Mattole Watershed Salmon Support Group became more successful at enhancing salmon populations and expanded its activities to include river restoration and rehabilitation projects, it became a topic of discourse within the group that a small number of people was now making decisions that affected the whole watershed. Some were allowing themselves to imagine a different sort of social organization. How would such an organization look, and how would it function? What was the practical geographical unit?

By the summer after the landslide, these concerns were widespread enough that a public meeting was convened.[2] Forty or so people attended the open-air gathering for a variety of reasons. Some wanted to see the benefits of more employment in what was coming to be recognized as the new field of watershed restoration. Most had reason to be concerned about their own access roads after the two wet winters. Many were angry about the steady pace of industrial logging aimed at liquidation of the last stands of ancient forest.

The discussion that continued all afternoon was dominated, however, by a growing mutual understanding. What would happen if we saw ourselves as common inhabitants of a naturally defined part of the planet rather than as members of competitive interest groups isolated from each other by property lines? A naturally defined area like, say, a watershed. Salmon had taught us that we live in watersheds, and the concept was no longer merely an abstraction. (Every person lives in one, and almost anybody, urban or rural, can see a ridgeline or watercourse somewhere in the course of his or her daily life.) As if to accommodate perceptual differences among people, a watershed organizes itself into ever more available scales—from river to tributary to swale. Any individual might be able to create a relationship with some small part of it. Neighborhood groups might be able to see their activities as a part of the function of a tributary basin. And thus we might build a community sensitive enough to understand and adjust itself to the opportunities and constraints of an even larger whole—in our case a riverine watershed of three hundred square miles.

What if we were to think of ourselves as operating within the time frame of geological processes and of the natural succession of ecological communities, rather than the quick wink of human generations or the even shorter fibrillations of political elections? How could we begin to act like people of a place rather than like consumers and producers in a market system over which we had little control? What if we began to develop and share our own vernacular experience and wisdom to the point where it had a credibility equal to that of the specialists in the state capital?

By the end of the afternoon, the Mattole Restoration Council (MRC) had been born, and its first newsletter was mailed in the fall of 1983 to every resident and landowner in the Mattole drainage. An article entitled "Why the Mattole Restoration Council?" presented the reader with a vision:

Imagine starting from the ridgetop and headwaters . . . planting trees and grasses for slope stability and future timber . . . as roads get built and maintained so that erosion slows rather than increases.

The river gradually flushes itself out and stabilizes. Vegetation begins to seal it in a cooling shade again. Work in salmon enhancement begins to pay off in visible increases in spawning runs. Silt washed off the upland slopes begins to deposit itself permanently in rich alluvial flats. Grains and vegetables grow in soil that was formerly swept out to sea.

A generation from now, our children reap a harvest of fine timber, abundant fish, productive grasslands and rich and varied plant and animal communities—but also a tradition that will assure the same harvest for their children.[3]

Who could fault such a program? We would find out as time went by.

"Belonging," writes Paul Shepard, building on psychologist Erik Erikson's work, "is the pivot of life, the point at which selfhood becomes possible—not just belonging in general, but in particular. One belongs to a universe of order and purpose that must initially be realized as a particular community of certain species in a terrain of unique geology."[4]

But too many of us come into a place and don't know how to be part of it, which is the same as saying we don't know where we are. Each biogeographical region presents a wonderful array of micro-climates, water flows, soil types, communities of flora and fauna. These are the very flesh and blood of place, and human beings have evolved to experience their relationship to the biosphere through sensual perception of these specific variations. But most of us have lost or been cut off from the skills of systematic attentiveness that open us to the natural world's instruction. We have forgotten how critical our connection with the particulars of place are to our social and cultural well-being. We have forgotten, or been deprived of, our history as human beings.

So often, instead, we come into a place assured by political ideologies and cultural conditioning that we are isolate individuals passing through. And yet we are deeply and inchoately troubled by feelings of dislocation, loneliness, and doubt. The very idea that we are free to act out our every notion backfires on us; we are encouraged by that same conditioning to blame ourselves for the social dysfunctions and ecological disruption we see around us. A great deal of that discomfort is generated by simply not knowing where we are.

The histories of nations and empires and the political and economic geographies memorialized in our schoolbooks do not give us the essential information we need to act our way into a working relationship with place. The history we need in order to make meaningful assessments of our collective options is the very history most often absent, most especially in America: the history embodied in the places where we are. The story a place has to tell, especially the story of the continuity of human presence in that place, is an absence so large in our culture as to be outside our range of vision. It is invisible like the air is invisible, but it is no less essential to our comfort and survival. The living region requires of us that we become its intimate inhabitants, and further, that we regrow our sense of community as a function of that inhabitation.

The history that will best serve the ends of learning to live as communities of place—to learn where we are—lies in the landscape surrounding us. The soil is made up of the flesh and bones of every creature who has passed this way in the last few millennia. Changes over time in particular landscapes can give us clues as to which styles of human occupation and interaction with the landscape have been in the interests of the health of the whole, and which have not. For such a study to have any meaning, we need to extend our sense of human continuity in any particular place back beyond the relatively recent arrival of industrial humans. It is up to us who are alive now to translate this information into something like the place's own memory.

From its beginnings in 1983, the Mattole Restoration Council became a fluid and dynamic coalition of member groups and individuals from various parts of the watershed. Some of the groups, like the Mattole Watershed Salmon Support Group, were already directly involved in salmon population and habitat work. Others were tributary stewardship groups made up of residents in a particular sub-basin. Two new land trusts signed on, each devoted to the preservation of local *refugia,* that is, remnants of forest and stream complexes that still have the self-organized characteristics of a wild and functional habitat. Still others were community service groups, local community centers, and the newly established independent high school. One group was set up as a worker-owned cooperative, a mobile unit of tree planters that could travel anywhere to service a contract requiring a trained crew. A seat on the MRC board of directors was assigned to represent individual membership—those watershed residents unaffiliated with any of the member groups, but who wanted to play a part.

Jan Morrison, a veteran of the tree planting co-ops that had proliferated like mushrooms in the seventies, was elected as chairwoman. Claire Trower, a schoolteacher, took on the thankless tasks of treasurer and bookkeeper. Randy Stemler, who had cut his landscape-rehabilitation teeth during the early, experimental years of the vast restoration effort of the Redwood National Park, contributed his skills in dealing with the tedium of contracts with public agencies, as well as a fastidiousness of mind that was a model for others new to the demands of contract bidding and the bitter adjustments that sometimes must be made to contain the work within a budget. Again, there was never enough money. I discovered in myself a shamelessness that enabled me to knock on the doors of foundations to ask them for money for a kind of work that had not yet entered the lexicon of social and environmental concerns.

Many of the people who attended the monthly meetings of the new organization were experiencing a small but important shift in their sense of relationship to the whole. Working together, with our feet in the water, moving large rocks and logs to armor raw and bleeding streambanks, or on the dry slopes above, planting trees, seemed to carry from our muscles to our minds a buried memory of human communities deeply integrated with the wild processes surrounding. To put it another way, such work satisfied the soul.

It became a primary goal of the Council to create more opportunities for this kind of hands-on engagement, by providing coordination and support for member group projects and by developing projects of its own. Over the next few years a whole range of contracts were implemented. The Coastal Headwaters Association, under the direction of Judi Quick and Richard Gienger, built a series of hand-placed rock structures along the headwaters of the mainstream, where the county road closely follows the course of the river, to protect against erosion. The structures were effective and so beautiful that they became a wellspring of community pride—artful sculptures in public places.

The Salmon Group supervised the construction of a large rip-rap structure along the lower reaches of the river, where it was eating away at its banks and threatening the county road. The project leaders, Jan Morrison and Randy Stemler, took willow and cottonwood cuttings and soaked them in water-filled plastic buckets in their backyards until they sprouted new roots. When the heavy equipment quit work each day, the two would scramble down the banks and tuck the rooted cuttings into the interstices between the boulders and rocks along the upper edge of the work that had been completed. The finished project redirected the scouring action of the river to its bottom, where it cut a deeper channel that could be used by juvenile fish, and shade from the growing cuttings cooled the water to provide a summertime sanctuary.

Through a combination of good luck and growing experience, most of the projects succeeded in accomplishing their limited goals, but some did not. Historical memory informed us that High Prairie Creek, a little tributary that passed under the county road, had once functioned as good salmon spawning habitat. A square concrete culvert built to get the creek under the road had increased the velocity of its flow and downcut the channel at the lower end of the structure, creating a waterfall that blocked the spawners, and the flat bottom of the culvert distributed the rushing flows of winter into a sheet of water too shallow for upstream migrants to negotiate even if they had been able to reach it. Gary Peterson took the best designs the Department of Fish and Game had to offer and improved on them. He supervised the construction of a small steel-reinforced concrete fish ladder up to the downstream edge of the culvert and a concrete curb down its center, which he designed to concentrate and deepen the flows on one side, to give the fish a passage deep enough to swim through. It should have worked, but the heavy flows over the next few winters moved large amounts of rubble through the culvert and destroyed the structures. Later we would discover that High Prairie Creek was in a very early phase of shaping its drainage; its slopes were one big earthflow that, once further destabilized by logging, would probably continue to violently rearrange itself for another two hundred years or so before the basin regained its dynamic equilibrium.

Such experiences reinforced—painfully—the recognition that we lacked a comprehensive understanding of the workings of the river system as a whole. But public land management agencies were still some years away from recognizing the value of whole-systems analysis, and they certainly weren't ready to release the large amount of funding that such an undertaking would require to a community of non-professionals.

The doorway to understanding that salmon had unlatched for a few of us had now swung open far enough so that anyone could wander through. One of those wanderers was a reporter from the *Los Angeles Times*.

Marijuana had come to be considered the number-one cash crop in California, and Humboldt County had gained some notoriety as a leading producer. The reporter was poking around through the Mattole in search of outlaw cultivation stories when he came upon a crew of volunteers marking hatchbox-reared fish for imminent release back into the river. The writer's curiosity was piqued. Here in the middle of the outlaw culture that was giving him such good copy he had stumbled across a nearly incomprehensible undertaking of an entirely different nature. That the volunteers were working in the rain must have further startled and impressed the newsman from rain-starved southern California. Gary explained to him what was going on and why. Once the *Times* had published its titillating series on renegade dope growers, the paper ran a story about this strange little group of good citizens in the backwoods, and ran it on the front page of the sports section.

In consequence, the telephone rang in my house one morning in the spring of 1985 and I picked up to find Gordon Van Vleck, Huey Johnson's successor in the office of state secretary of resources, on the other end of the line. Evidently it was Mr. Van Vleck's habit to read the sports section of the *Los Angeles Times* with his coffee first thing in the morning, and he wanted to know why he had never heard of us before. Dazedly, I stumbled through an explanation of what we thought we were up to. Well, what did we need? he asked. Money, I said flatly, too groggy and surprised to run through the usual litany about the importance of our work to the people of California. After a pause, Secretary Van Vleck wondered out loud if there might not be some unappropriated cash left in the languishing Renewable Resource Investment Fund established by his predecessor. If he could find it, how much did we need and how would we use it? I said I would get back to him.

A few calls to the most active people of the MRC to determine priorities produced a uniform set of responses. The pressing need for some sort of comprehensive assessment of current watershed processes was widely recognized, but so was the need to protect the remaining refugia. Some of the fragments of stable forest and stream habitat thus far spared from conversion into product and profit were on public lands, and protection for those could be pursued through political channels. But many more were on lands owned by one or another of the four industrial timberland owners in the watershed. There seemed no other method to preserve these places than to buy them outright, an alarmingly expensive prospect even when the owners were willing to sell.

One such fragment had been identified as critical to the downstream survival of coho salmon: the Mill Creek Forest, 220 steep acres that included the largest stand of ancient trees remaining in the lower river valley. There were valid arguments that it was not large enough by itself to continue to provide for the needs of the terrestrial species it had once been home to, but no one doubted that its stabilizing and cooling effect on Mill Creek was the reason that this stream was the only tributary in the lower valley still capable of supporting coho salmon.

By afternoon I was able to return Secretary Van Vleck's call. We needed a hundred thousand dollars, I said, trying to sound confident. Very well, the Resources Agency would accept a proposal. Eight months later we had contracts for the entire amount, to be split equally between the MRC, for an inventory of the largest sources of sedimentation in the river watershed, and the Mill Creek Watershed Conservancy, a backyard land trust that had been established for the purpose of pursuing the acquisition of the Mill Creek Forest.

"We cannot live in a community that is interpreted for us by others," writes political scientist Michael McGinnis. "An interpreted community is not home."[5]

The Mattole Restoration Council, faced with a choice of hiring professionals to do the job or training resident non-

professionals, made a conscious decision to go with the locals. Either option would cost about the same, and we reasoned that if the work was done by watershed residents it
would produce something more than data; it would generate
skills in systematic attentiveness to the larger patterns in the
backyard landscape. The effort was localized even further by
dividing the drainage into twelve contiguous sub-basin
areas. Teams of surveyors were mobilized and trained. Landscape history and assessment of current conditions, when
pursued from a home embedded in that same landscape,
loses its remote and abstract quality. The ever-deepening layers of interpretation became almost instantly embodied as an
element of creek-by-creek culture.

Terry Spreiter, head geologist for Redwood National
Park, drove down on weekends to help us work out a stan-
dardized methodology. She and David Burnson, a park geo-
morphologist turned heavy-equipment operator, conducted
training sessions in aerial photo interpretation and map-
making skills. The Council rented a tiny office in the attic of
the community center in the downstream hamlet of Petrolia. From there a sort of treasure hunt was organized.

The materials we needed in order to paint a picture of the
watershed as a fluid interpenetration of human activities and
the place's own processes resided in dozens of far-flung dusty
filing cabinets. The earliest aerial photos of the region, taken
in 1942, were kept in the National Archives in Virginia.
Later photos were scattered all over the county—in the local
office of the Bureau of Land Management, at the county Department of Public Works, in the map room of the local state
university. The names and addresses of landowners were all
in the county assessor's office; they were filed not by location
but by parcel number. (In that office, a treasure was found
that none of us knew existed, a timber harvest history of the

area gathered between 1960 and 1972, the years during
which the onerous tax on standing timber had been collected.) The river arises in one county and flows into another, requiring travel to one county seat fifty miles to the
north and another a hundred and fifty miles to the south. The
watershed was also divided into two separate regional juris-
dictions of the Department of Fish and Game and the Department of Forestry: more travels, more phone calls.

The project took three years to complete and generated three products.

The first was a database reorganized into creek-specific
maps and addresses for watershed residents, which allowed
the MRC to communicate with specific resident populations
about those issues which affected them most directly. The so-
called NIMBY ("Not In My Back Yard") phenomenon so
abhorrent to national environmental organizations was never
seen by the Council as an obstacle, but rather as a natural
manifestation of the limits of human perception and extended identity. Why not think of it as a tool through which
to transform individual anxieties into community mobili-
zation?

The second result of these explorations was a dramatically
graphic poster map of the watershed which compared the
extent of the distribution of old-growth forests in 1947 (just
at the beginning of the timber boom) with the 9 percent remaining in 1988 and pointed out that almost none of the
remaining ancient forest had any legal protection. The timber wars had been heating up as we worked, most of the conflict revolving around the defense of ancient forests. As we'd
listened to the passionate rhetoric of the enviros, the high-
handed rebuttals of the timber industry, and the confused responses of regulatory agencies, we'd come to realize that no

one knew exactly how much ancient forest was actually out there. (A little later, the U.S. Forest Service found itself with the same problem.)

Time after time, salmon workers had experienced directly the interlocking relationship between the health of forests and the health of the salmon, and every local survey had documented the benefit of the cooling, stabilizing, and sediment-filtering qualities of older, undamaged forests. Ludicrously, though, the relationship between salmon survival and old forests was still a political hot potato; every academic study that demonstrated this synergistic relationship would generate a new academic study, contracted from the same labor pool of professional biologists and geologists, that showed no relationship whatsoever; for thirty years both the courts and the public had remained confused by conflicting "expert" testimony and the land-use agencies had been paralyzed.

The MRC poster, mailed to every Mattole resident and landowner, as well as to regulatory agencies, had an electrifying impact. (For years I would see it posted in bureaucratic offices, at the headquarters of industrial timber companies, and on the walls of backwoods cabins in the home place.) The short text on the back of the poster did not try to resolve the argument about salmon and old-growth forests, but simply pointed to the long-term economic consequences of short-term exploitation of forest resources in terms of the ability of resident landowners to support themselves in the future. The headline, in eighteen-point type, read, "In the Mattole River watershed, only nine percent of old-growth forests remain standing. Second growth is fifty years away from maturity. Where do we go from here?"

The poster became a tool in a considerable portfolio of strategies held by Rondal Snodgrass, director of the recently formed Sanctuary Forest, a land trust dedicated to the formation of a large ecological reserve in the headwaters of the Mattole. In the face of a vigorous media campaign by the timber industry to discredit the very idea of preservation, Rondal would hold fast to what seemed at the time to be a nearly unimaginable goal: creating a contiguous reserve of a thousand uncut acres of mixed redwood and Douglas-fir around that portion of the river where the largest number of king salmon prefer to spawn each year. In a campaign strategy that would come to include demonstrations, civil disobedience, lawsuits, and prayer vigils with the sisters at the Redwood Monastery, Rondal used the map and the message to demonstrate the need to potential public and private donors of the enormous amounts of money his group's efforts would require.

Other communities were quick to use the poster to pick out the remnant forests closest to home and begin to ponder their future. Due to the efforts of a community organized around Gilham Butte, a smaller parcel of BLM-managed old growth on the eastern boundary of the watershed, the MRC map played some small role in that agency's 1988 decision to create an Old Growth Reserve System in northern California, and it was also used by the Mill Creek Watershed Conservancy in its struggle to protect the Mill Creek Forest in the face of rapidly escalating timber prices.

In my mind, however, the map held a significance that went beyond preservationist goals. For the first time, all the inhabitants of the watershed had a common reference point from which to consider their undeniably related futures.

The third product of the MRC's information gathering was a forty-eight-page tabloid titled *Elements of Recovery* and featuring even more detailed maps of the largest sources of sedimentation to the river system. Terry Spreiter's consultation had led us to catalog disturbances in four general categories: surface erosion, gullies, landslides, and trashed channels (the latter a particularly descriptive technical term for streams that have lost their border of riparian vegetation due to sediment-induced flooding). The tabloid also contained detailed timber harvest maps of the twelve sub-basins the MRC had identified, descriptions of the geological processes that had formed each basin, a cultural history of the valley, and a glossary of technical jargon.

The daunting process of preparing this document may have also been, for the restorationists involved, its most rewarding effect. They learned which landslides could be treated and which could not. They gained a fuller picture of the dynamic processes of disturbance and recovery in watercourses, one which would allow them to design and locate future projects to optimum effect. They began to understand that the survival of open space depends on the ability of resident landowners to hold together the larger parcels, which in turn depends on the parcels remaining economically productive. Perhaps most importantly, the project took place over a long enough period of time so that the amazing resilience of natural systems could be experienced firsthand.

The most revelatory of these experiences of the healing powers of nature involved the trashed channels. The primary inventory tool was a set of aerial photos taken in 1984 and enlarged to a scale of one inch to four hundred feet. Nineteen eighty-four marked the end of a two-year flood cycle brought on by El Niño and the beginning of a seven-year drought cycle during which winter rainfall averages fell far below normal. The photos provided a dramatic picture of miles of overloaded tributaries whose banks had been denuded by the recent floods. The trashed channels crawled like an infestation of worms all over the fastidious translation of the photos into charts sketched on tracing paper. The protocol was to map the disturbances that could be identified and prioritize them for field inspection based on whether or not the sediment sources might lend themselves to prescriptive treatment and on the willingness of landowners to allow us access. Surveyors didn't get into the field until 1988, four years into the drought.

The most direct route to inspect the channels often lay right up the waterways themselves. It sometimes took hours of rock-hopping and bushwhacking to arrive at the disturbances that had been so carefully mapped. The people doing the field checking were adept in the use of map and compass; they sometimes also carried copies of the original photos with them, carefully rolled into tubes that stuck out of their backpacks and got hung up on low branches. The trashed channels should have been easy to find. The barren areas that had shown up glaringly on the photos were often miles long and as much as a hundred yards wide. You should have been able to know you were there when you emerged from the shade of less damaged reaches into long stretches of bright sunlight that would be heating up the water in the disturbed areas.

But with few exceptions, the trashed channels could not be found. Everywhere they should have been, there were thickets of red alder grown to a height of four to twenty feet. The initial response was one of unsettling dumfoundment. Were we lost? Had our compasses somehow become demagnetized? Had we failed to reckon correctly the distances we had traveled? A flurry of puzzled phone consultations soon revealed the answer. The landscape was showing us one of the ways it healed itself.

The seed cones of the red alder, along with willow the

most common tree sheltering the waterways, each contain
many thousands of tiny seeds. The cones ripen and spread
open to release their seeds at about the same time the first
winter rains roll in. The cones fall into the rushing streams
and drift into quiet back eddies where they lodge themselves
in freshly exposed soils as the water level drops. There they
sprout to grow exuberantly. Red alder can put on as much
as four feet of annual new growth when the conditions are
just right.

In flood years, when the waters stay high for an extended
period, the seed cones are likely to be swept into the river
and out to sea, and many of the smaller seedlings that have
established themselves in recent drier years are torn out and
carried away along with the cones. But in drier years, when
the seasonal rains are broken by periods of drought, the waters rise and fall more frequently and more gently: more of
the seed cones remain in the drainage of their origin. During
a series of drought years, a commonplace pattern in California, the alders and willows are able to grow to a size that may
be able to hold against the force of the higher waters that
come the next year or the next. And this is the phenomenon
that we were witnessing.

The initial confusion was experienced individually. But
the revelation of its meaning was a collective experience that
produced one of those tiny shifts in perception that can make
a large difference in how you conduct your life. The watershed was healing itself, and doing so at a rate that our most
grandiose ambitions could never come near to emulating.
The discovery gentled us as a group, moved us to a humility of purpose for which we could only be grateful. The Earth
would heal itself. We could either move away entirely for
two hundred years, or we could make the processes of recovery our guide and seek to put our hand in wherever it would

effectively move the process along. We were rediscovering
that all learning is collaborative and that the collaboration
extends beyond humans to the landscape and the many intel-
ligences embedded therein.

🐟 Maps are magical icons. We think of them as pictures
of an objective reality, but they are talismans that twist our
psyches in one direction or another. We use them hoping for
help in finding our way around unknown territory; we hope
they will guide us in the right direction. We are hardly aware
of the ways in which they are prescribing the way we think
of ourselves and of our extended identities.

The Mattole Restoration Council's mapping work produced the rough beginning of a picture of some of the nonhuman aspects of our human home—the condition of drainage
patterns and how they affected the condition of salmon populations, the condition of the forest and how it affected
everything. But the MRC found another pattern as well: the
way that the distribution of property affected the future of
the watershed landscape.

By 1988, property boundaries sliced up the 306-square-
mile Mattole watershed into 2,680 parcels owned by 910
separate entities. These lines cut natural habitats and streams
into disconnected pieces that defined the limits of our intimacy with the land; they fragmented the perceptions of resident humans. The dim blue lines on yellowed paper in
county assessors' offices everywhere are like laser knives that
disconnect our domesticated minds from the wild habit of
water to flow downhill, from the uses of the whole of a
stream by aquatic creatures, from the migration patterns of
terrestrial animals, and from the fluid response of plant communities to minute changes in soil and climate and water.
They disconnect us from each other. Unless the Council

learned to relate to each of those 9 1 0 individuals and institutions on their own terms—as expressed in their perceived
needs and land-use practices—its growing understanding of
landscape-scaled processes of disturbance and recovery
would be incomplete.

The salmon had brought us this far. We would be left
to our own devices to deal with our own kind.

It invariably turns out, I think, that one's first vision of one's place was to some extent an imposition on it. But if one's sight is clear and if one stays on and works well, one's love gradually responds to the place as it really is, and one's visions gradually imagine possibilities that are really in it. Vision, possibility, work, life—all have changed by mutual correction.

WENDELL BERRY, *Standing by Words*

LIKE MOST PLACES in the American West, the Mattole River basin has experienced three waves of change in the last hundred and fifty years, each of which has carried with it a different set of relationships between the life of the place and the lives and livelihoods of its human population. The details vary from place to place, but the pattern remains uniform: occupation of the land by various people acting out the Euro-American doctrine of Manifest Destiny so rapidly and violently as to effect a nearly total break in the cultural continuity of the human presence; quickly exhausted economies based on centralized extractive industries in the century that followed; and, more recently, a wave of new immigrants fleeing the failures of urban centers to provide them with security and community. In different ways in different places, this latter, most recent pulse of settlement defines the arena for a struggle to learn at last where we are and to understand the terms of obligation such recognition might entail.

The first white settlement in the Mattole drainage was not established until 1857, by a disappointed gold miner named Alfred Augustus Hadley. Hadley was soon followed by others, most of whom brought cattle with them—cattle that would become the keystone for a rapidly developing new subsistence economy as well as provide the rationalization for the ferocity of their conflict with the indigenous people who had lived in the area for a thousand or more years. By 1862, almost all of the Mattole and Sinkyone people who inhabited the Mattole Valley had been killed in battle, murdered by vigilantes, or removed to either the Round Valley Reservation (a hundred miles to the southeast) or the larger Hoopa Reservation (an equal distance to the northeast). Individuals did, of course, escape and drift back to the homelands that were an essential part of their identities, and it was the descendants of those bereft people that anthropologists interviewed one and two generations later. These scanty notations are the only clues remaining to us to bridge an otherwise total discontinuity in the long experience of human habitation of the place.[1]

The indigenous peoples had actively managed the coastal forests for acorn production, burning through them judiciously to clean the forest floor and control insect infestation. The random incidence of wildfires that are an essential part of the ecology of the open coastal and ridgetop prairies was also augmented by occasional purposeful burns, which maintained these perennial bunchgrass prairies as grazing habitat for deer and elk, another important food source. The annual pulse of salmon that came as a gift from the sea required little management beyond the establishment of community standards of behavior; the recognition of the need to honor the nature of the gift was embodied in annual ceremonies, celebrations, and rites of self-regulation.

The new arrivals managed the land for cattle and sheep production. They too burned, but now they were burning and expanding prairies that had suffered conversion to annual European grasses, the seeds of which had been carried in the hooves of their imported livestock. Native bunchgrasses, with their large root masses, had tended to provide year-round nutrition for the ungulates that grazed them, but the annual exotics stop growing and lose their nutritive value in the dry summers of California. The few alluvial flatlands were plowed and planted to hay crops that were now needed to get the settlers' livestock through lean seasons. The Douglas-fir forest that encroached on the prairies was laboriously cut and the timber simply left at the edges of the expanded pastureland.

Few of the new occupants learned to enjoy acorns as food; they planted to wheat the rare flatlands that were not needed to produce hay for their livestock. The ubiquitous tan oak provided a supplementary income in the form of tannin extracted from its bark to cure leather. A small but important industry in tanbark was pursued by cutting down as large a tract of the trees as double-bitted axes and crosscut saws would allow, stripping their bark, and leaving the wood behind.

It was a good life for a people who quickly grew self-sufficient, but it was more labor-intensive than old ways had been. In his memoirs, T. K. Clark describes the work ethic that brought to the land changes few in his generation ever thought to question: "The Indians were great for sitting around on their haunches and letting the days go by but they knew if they sat around all the time that soon they would have fat bucks to feed on." As for the white settlers, "You can believe that if they didn't do the feeding no one else was obligated to do it for them. No food stamps, no welfare checks to be had, just for the asking. Every family had a father who was the provider of the necessary food and clothing. If the necessities of life were short, the man of the house worked longer hours and the mother did the same. No one loafed as I can remember."[2] In the converted landscape, fewer people were working longer hours to gain a level of subsistence comparable to that of the culture they had replaced.

But the new people brought with them something less tangible that changed the landscape as extensively as the cattle and sheep and alien grasses would—the notion of absolute dominion over the land. Ideas rule the American West, says writer Anne Matthews, and always have.[3]

Sometimes history shapes itself into a parable. Consider the Gregg-Wood expedition. The party of exploration led by Dr. Josiah Gregg and Lewis K. Wood is among the three or four that are credited with the "discovery" of Humboldt Bay, some thirty coastwise miles to the north of the mouth of the Mattole River. (Humboldt Bay would later become the most active commercial port in California north of San Francisco.) Gregg was a scientist, a geological surveyor employed by the federal government to chart some of the new territory that was about to become the state of California. Wood was an experienced land speculator and developer who had bought and sold lots in the sleepy village of San Jose before he was drawn to the Trinity River country to prospect for gold; later in life, he would become the first Recorder of Deeds in Humboldt County, in Uniontown on Humboldt Bay.

Eight men left the Trinity on November 5, 1849, outfitted for a ten-day journey to seek out the body of protected water rumored to be that far to the west. Their informants may have been Hupa people who knew the trails to the coast, but

Gregg cared nothing for the trails—he chose rather to follow the tools of his trade, the sextant, the quadrant, and the surveyor's level. The tools did what they do best and led the party in a straight line over some of the most tortuous terrain in northern California. After more than a month of lugging Gregg's heavy equipment up and down one steep ridge after another, the party emerged, starving and desperate, at exactly the point Gregg had predicted—at latitude 41 degrees north. Gregg may have been pleased, but most of the men in the party had grown an abiding hatred for his methods.

The men found Humboldt Bay, but they had lost interest in the project; they wanted only to find a way south, to the provisions of Santa Rosa. At a river near flood stage just north of the bay, some natives, probably Wiyot people, offered to ferry the men across. When Gregg asked the party to wait while he set up his tools to establish their celestial location, the request initiated an altercation of such fury that it is memorialized in the name the river bears today: the Mad. The party split in two, one group under the leadership of Lewis Wood, a few men sticking with Gregg and his sextant. Gregg headed west and refound the coast at Cape Mendocino, but was turned inland again by the difficulty of the mountains south of the Mattole; he died of starvation before he reached Santa Rosa. The Wood party headed south along the lush alluvial valley of the lower Eel River. Wood survived, but not before he had been mauled severely by a grizzly bear.

Hadley family lore has it that during one of the several scouting expeditions that would lead to A. A. Hadley's eventual settlement in the Mattole, he encountered the Wood party just after the separation. Hadley sketched a map for Wood, so the story goes, which eventually got Wood's group back to civilization. If the story is true, the two men were together within days of a brooding journal entry made by

Wood shortly before the parties parted so bitterly. Wood's note, written from the depths of physical desperation, might serve as an anthem illuminating the collective state of mind that allowed the North American West to be treated as a resource colony for the next century: "One and all declared they would no longer lend assistance to man or beast and from this forward each would constitute a company by himself, under obligations to no one and free to act as best suited his notions."[4] The ghost of John Locke seems condemned to wander the lands he so unwisely described as empty.

Property is religion in America, if religion can be defined as the body of faith that informs community standards of moral decision. As Donald Worster has observed, "Private property in land more or less appeared and grew up as America did, and we Americans have believed in that institution more than any other people on earth. In fact it may be our most cherished institution."[5] This institution had been elevated to a natural right some three hundred years ago by the aforementioned Enlightenment philosopher John Locke, and transformed into a cornerstone of American identity by a visionary Thomas Jefferson.

"God, who hath given the world to men in common," wrote Locke, "hath also given them reason to make use of it to the best advantage of life and convenience. The earth and all that is therein is given to men for the support and comfort of their being. And though all the fruits it naturally produces, and the beasts it feeds, belong to mankind in common . . . there must of necessity be some way or other [of establishing ownership] before they can become of any use, or at all beneficial, to any particular men."[6] Jefferson imbued that natural right with the highest of virtue, at least as it might be assumed by independent landowners dispersed across the landscape: "Those who labor in the earth are the chosen people of God, if ever he had a chosen people, whose breast he has made his peculiar deposit for substantial and genuine virtue. It is the focus in which he keeps alive that sacred fire, which otherwise might escape from the earth."[7]

Both Locke's and Jefferson's thinking was in part inspired by the "emptiness" of the North American landscape that they imagined to be so vast as to be inexhaustible. Locke was aware that Europe was already overcrowded and used the "wasted lands" in America, which he had never seen, to demonstrate the infinite potential that drove his logic of property and commodity. Locke declared that the highest function of government was the protection of the private property of the commoner, a revolutionary concept in a time when dominion over property had been considered the exclusive domain of the aristocracy.

Jefferson's revolutionary thinking was powerfully influenced by Locke's, but he gave it his own spin. Jefferson was in the business of *creating* private property. During his presidency, he was faced with the thrilling challenge of developing huge acquisitions of land by the new American nation, territories that compared in size to all of Europe. Among the first things he did in regard to the newly acquired lands was to send out surveyors who would impose on their entirety a pattern of grids called townships and ranges and sections, the cadastral survey that frames the terms of every real estate transaction today. Jefferson saw this work as a necessary first step in bringing order to a sprawling "wilderness." The tidy squares superimposed on the map of areas few new Americans had ever seen was a pattern designed to expedite their hasty occupation by the yeoman farmer-democrats that the president saw as the chosen people of God. If the new government was to have something to govern, it needed to transform all of that land into property.

Neither Locke nor Jefferson could have imagined a time

when the North American continent would be so fully occupied as to interrupt the migration of birds and fishes and bison; neither could imagine the massive extinctions of species that would accompany conquest. (In fact, throughout his life Jefferson maintained an interpretation of nature so perfectly balanced that the extinction of a species was not conceivable.) Certainly neither of them imagined that corporate entities would one day be invested with privileges similar to those held by the aristocracy in the seventeenth and eighteenth centuries—the very privileges their theories were meant to subvert. Nevertheless, a great deal of the two men's thinking on the issue of land as property was lodged in the hearts and minds of my twentieth-century neighbors as fundamental articles of faith, even though few of us have sat down to study Jefferson's writings and even fewer have read Locke's.

It is not difficult to understand why a philosophy three hundred years old, and the revolutionary theories it informed, are still embraced so passionately in our own times. Nineteenth-century federal laws like the Pre-emption Act of 1841 and the later Homestead Act of 1860 made available an opportunity that had never existed before—the illusion of free land. Tens of thousands of hardy people headed west to try their hands at the rough self-sufficiency and family security that the title to a piece of land might offer. If the first try didn't work out—and a very large number of them didn't— well, then, move on and try again. The land filled up with Euro-Americans in a steady westward progression that finally reached our westernmost edge of the continent in 1849, less than half a century before historian Frederick Jackson Turner would declare the frontier gone.

By the time they had reached the limit of their expansion, these pioneers were a toughened and savvy breed. They had learned important lessons about the skills of self-sufficiency from the failed experiments that littered the landscape behind them: prairies plowed up and then abandoned, sod huts melting back into the soil. Most of them had been drawn to California by the Gold Rush, an experience that must have reinforced their conviction that the only true source of stability and survival was vested in a secured land base. They must have been aware, too, that this farthest edge of the continent might represent their last chance at realizing their dreams, an awareness which would go a long way toward explaining the brutal efficiency with which the white settlers of all of northwest California dispatched their indigenous predecessors.[8]

The new maps drawn and distributed by the MRC in the late 1980s were not meant to undermine the foundations of the house of security and self-determination that the well-worked privately owned parcel of land provides. Many of the mappers were new property owners themselves, though most of their holdings were small, and few of them shared the hard-earned skills embodied by the descendants of those first white settlers. The strategy of the maps was rather to evoke an arena for collective perception and cooperative planning—a context that might assure some continuation of the dream of a fulfilling life taken from a bountiful landscape.

Before the end of World War II, much of the land base had been controlled by the descendants of the area's white pioneers. They and their fathers and grandmothers had led a hard but rewarding life. They could depend on their neighbors to help out with the intense seasonal work that attended cattle-sorting or sheepshearing or home-canning at harvest time.

They could also depend on their neighbors to treat each

others' ranches as if they were sovereign entities. Privately they might not approve of some sloppy aspect of a neighbor's land management, but an unspoken code of honor forbade them from holding any public opinion about the management of another's property: If your neighbor has no right to criticize your use of your land, neither do you have a right to criticize theirs. Again, the ghost of John Locke speaks: "For as a man had a right to all he could employ his labour upon, so he had no temptation to labour for more than he could make use of. This left no room for controversy about the title, nor for the encroachment upon the right of others."[9]

As we have seen, some of those neighbors *had* been tempted by the promises of wealth held out by industrial-style timber extraction, and the ensuing logging boom *had* encroached on the rights of others, if only in the floods of rubble that filled the streams of adjacent properties downstream. But no matter. The articles of faith embedded in Worster's "most cherished institution" proved stronger than the evidence of the senses.

In the early 1970s another temptation came along. When a few of the ranchland owners compared the prices that developers were offering for northern California land with the subsistence income that ranching provided, they decided to sell their logged-over lands to the developers. Love of their land was still the strongest glue binding the community together, and only a few betrayed this trust—for it *was* experienced as a betrayal by the majority who decided to hang tough. But ranchland holdings tend to run to the thousands of acres, and it took the breakup of only a few of them, combined with attractive terms offered by a local developer, to set off a new invasion—the one of which I and many of the other "new settlers" were a part. Stretches of the Mattole and surrounding drainages became a target destination for young back-to-the-landers who were leaving urban America in droves. In a little over ten years the population of the basin tripled.

The newcomers must have seemed nearly as strange—and their cultural attitudes as uniform and threatening—as the original Euro-Americans had appeared to the indigenous Mattole and Sinkyone peoples. The new invaders *looked* wrong. The men wore their hair too long; all dressed in Salvation Army hand-me-downs; they let their babies run around naked. They smoked marijuana like a normal person would drink beer. They didn't have the right attitudes toward work. And they wandered all over the place. In the early days of the hegira, at least, most of the newcomers were likely to be more sympathetic to Rebecca Solnit's aphorism about property—"a person can be said to own land in much the same way that a flea owns its dog"[10]—than they were to John Locke's logic. And there were so *many* of them. Not only did every last one of them seem to be an environmentalist, but they were arrogant about it. They knew nothing of the courtesies of the old code of silence, and they felt free to criticize a style of land management they as yet knew very little about.

While a considerable number of the old-timers were curious about and generous to the new people, much of the traditional community retreated into isolated enclaves where resentment could grow undisturbed. With a few very notable exceptions, always among individuals, there was little communication between the two populations, both of which were anarchist to the bone. The ranchers had little taste for meetings or for speaking in public. The newcomers had endless meetings, but these rarely resulted in any collective decision. There had been few attempts at rapprochement. Most back-to-the-landers were so entranced by their vision of creating a new world that they remained blissfully unaware of the effect they were having on the people whose ways of life they had disrupted so thoroughly.

From their beginnings, however, both the Salmon Group and the Mattole Restoration Council had understood that all residents of the area were natural allies for their ambitions. The older population knew the stories that could provide what scientists like to call baseline data. The best of them were careful land managers; they knew each twist and turn of the tumbled landscape and the vagaries of the seasons in the deep way that can only come from lifelong observation. They embodied those qualities of character that Italian journalist Luigi Barzini once described as residing in the "humble skills of men who have to work with lackadaisical unpredictable nature, the skills . . . of sailors, fishermen, farmers, horsetamers, the people who must at all cost avoid deceiving .themselves and must develop prudence, skepticism, resignation, as well as great fortitude and patience."[11]

Brothers John and Russell Chambers, fourth-generation ranchers, were active in their support of the fledgling Salmon Group; one of the group's several trapping sites was located on the ranch of one of the oldest pioneer families; and Allen Miner, descended from another pioneer family (and in his late seventies the master of the local Grange), sat through the first year of long Council organizational meetings and advised the group as to how to make itself credible to the wider community. But for the most part the ranchland owners watched in skeptical silence and the restoration groups continued to draw most of their energy and workforce from the more recently arrived settlers.

But lessons learned during the mapping process brought the importance of the survival of the ranching community into sharp relief for the MRC. Most species of wildlife need large open spaces to maintain genetic health as well as viable levels of population. With the exception of lands dedicated to intensive timber production, ranchland under almost any sort of management requires fewer fences, fewer structures, and fewer roads than land used for other human purposes. The MRC's mapping effort showed that over 70 percent of the large erosion problems in the watershed were related to poorly designed roads. Most Council members believed that the survival of the ranching tradition was a necessary element in any dream of maintaining the wild.

Besides the prairie lands dedicated to rangeland production, which made up a quarter of the Mattole land base, another 12 percent was overseen by the Bureau of Land Management under a benign management category—national conservation area—which had been created by Congress in 1972. Although agency professionals had been somewhat hostile early on to the watershed-scaled ambitions of the Mattole restoration groups, there were institutional avenues along which to press for their continued management of these lands as open spaces.[12]

While only another 12 percent of the watershed was managed by four industrial timber companies, the MRC's research revealed that these holdings were excruciatingly important to any hope of sustaining biological diversity: nearly half of the remaining old-growth forests, along with the whole range of species that depend on that stage of ecological succession for their survival, were on industrial lands. All four companies were land-based, which was good; one could appeal to their need for sustained production in the attempt to move them in the direction of management for wildlife and watershed values. Two of them were medium-sized and regionally based, which was also good; we could expect them to be at least somewhat responsive to the concerns of their neighbors.

But corporations are corporations. They make no pretense of living anywhere, and even a land-based corporation is unlikely to consider any one part of its holdings as important to anything but the requirement that it maintain a steady cash flow to its stockholders. While corporate managers could credibly maintain that their large clear-cuts would grow back eventually, we knew such practices have the effect of extirpating local wildlife populations forever.

The largest Mattole timberland owner was the Pacific Lumber Company, which in 1985 had been swallowed up by the Maxxam Corporation in a hostile takeover. Maxxam, with its headquarters in Houston, Texas, was known for its total dedication to the bottom line and would certainly consider its ancient forests in the Mattole as expendable as cans of tuna on a grocery store shelf. The largest, and therefore most viable, remnant stand of old-growth Douglas-fir forest was located on Maxxam land—three thousand acres of it in the headwaters of the North Fork and the Upper North Fork, the two largest tributaries of the river.

The remaining half of the watershed land base was now held by smaller landowners; about half of these resided on their land and half were absentee owners. In terms of population, this group of small landowners represented some 95 percent of the total number of property owners in the basin.[13] The new arrivals had increased the population of the valley to something over two thousand people, and their presence constituted the most recent large-scale conversion of the landscape. Their smaller parcels had further fragmented previously open space, and the developers had hastily pushed hundreds of miles of new access roads through the steep hills, usually following the faint tracks of old logging roads that were often perilously situated.

While many of the new settlers had originally shared a sense of community and some loosely defined vision of co-operative living, that vision had begun to fray, partly as a result of yet another new economy based on global market forces—the large-scale marijuana cultivation that attracted our *L.A. Times* reporter. By the early 1980s this economy had become so large and pervasive that the state came to consider it a threat to its tax-based integrity. The Campaign Against Marijuana Propagation (CAMP) was a paramilitary cooperation between state and federal law enforcement agencies that filled the skies with helicopters each August and September. The presence of a common enemy in the form of an annual invasion by the state might have reunified the community. But the price of the powerful *sensemilla* had risen to two thousand dollars a pound, and the most notable effect of CAMP was to keep it rising. Locked gates appeared everywhere, as a defense against both the on-the-ground maneuvers of the law and the growing incidence of crop theft. Neighbors no longer told each other the truth. It was a new gold rush, and defensive distrust eroded the community's sense of itself, in yet another strange iteration of John Locke's philosophy.

Scientific thinking has convinced us that the loftiest aspiration of rationality is objectivity, which implies that humans are capable of removing themselves—or some purely mental part of themselves—from the body of life that is the context not only for their individuality but for their very existence. But each individual is an assemblage of attitudes, personal and genetic histories, and unique capabilities and disabilities that keep them equidistant from the lofty—and finally unattainable—goal of objectivity. A place is an amalgam of subjectivities. Quakers have a saying to describe this phenomenon: "Each person holds a piece of the truth." Carry this thought into an ecological view of the world and it becomes "Each creature holds (an exquisitely vital) piece of the truth." We are indeed many pairs of eyes peering at each other out of the same living body, as David Abram had said.

To engage the place is to engage the challenge of building a community of place that includes each creature and every human neighbor. Passions born of such communion might generate the only moral authority powerful enough to deflect the voracious appetites of a global economy based only on the principles of production and consumption.

It is one thing to catalog the conditions of the landscape. It is a more ambitious undertaking to convince one's neighbors that such a picture is the rough sketch of a common territory, an invitation to explore a more inclusive security based on their cohabitation with each other and the larger patterns of life surrounding. Wallace Stegner has written,

Cultural differentiation takes a long time, and happens most completely in isolation and to homogeneous peoples, as happened to the Paiutes. The West has had neither time nor isolation nor homogeneity of race and occupation. Change, both homegrown and imported, has overtaken, time and again. We have to adapt not only to our changed physical environment but to our own adaptations, and sometimes we have to backtrack from our own mistakes.

Forming cultures involving heterogeneous populations do not grow steadily from definable quality to definable quality. Not only is their development complicated by class, caste, and social mobility, but they undergo simultaneous processes of erosion and deposition. They start from something, not from nothing. Habits and attitudes that have come to us embedded in our inherited culture, especially our inherited language, come incorporated in everything from nursery rhymes to laws and prayers, and they often have the durability of flint pebbles in puddingstone. No matter how completely their old matrix is dissolved, they remain intact, and are deposited almost unchanged in the strata of the new culture.[14]

The MRC's evocative maps of the watershed were the hopeful projection—for some of the people who lived within it—of the puddingstone of an emergent place-based culture. The pie chart that revealed the larger categories of land-use distribution was a picture of contentious groupings of cultural attitudes *about* land use: the flint pebbles within the stone.

Corporate ambitions generate their own large weather systems, which sweep through a region like devastating rain, and the runoff from these storms cuts down through the social strata to make the lines that separate them vividly apparent. Ineffective attempts by big government to mitigate the impact of that devastation and the energetic work of environmentalists to make governments more responsive collide with a predictable regularity like seasonal hurricanes of a ferocity that can make one forget the cycle of seasons in place.

In the ten years that the Salmon Group had worked to enhance and monitor native salmon populations, the number of returning spawners had continued to fall until it reached a nadir of an estimated two hundred kings in 1990. The extreme cycles of flood and drought during that decade had combined to amplify the delayed effects of the logging boom of twenty years earlier. The floods had continued to bring down the spoils left from failed roads and landings to destroy salmon habitat; the five years of drought that followed had stranded the spawning fish in the lower reaches of the river. Even though close to a quarter of a million healthy juveniles that might not have otherwise survived had been released back into the wild by the Salmon Group, the spawning run had continued to decline. But now the decline had credible documentation provided by the group's annual carcass counts, and those numbers were on the desks of Department of Fish and Game biologists.

Combined with the recently released maps of the Mattole Restoration Council, those numbers had changed the status of the river system from one that had been written off by wildlife managers ten years before to one that could no longer be ignored. In an unprecedented move, Banky Curtis, chief of the DFG region that includes most of the river system, released a memorandum which recommended that henceforth all logging operations in the drainage result in net zero contribution of sediment to the river and no increase in water temperatures. This recommendation, in the context of tensions already generated by the listing of the Northern spotted owl, an old-growth-dependent bird, as an endangered species, served to polarize a community that had by this time evolved a sort of peaceful, if distant, coexistence.

Although the restorationists had tried to avoid assigning blame for the damages they were cataloging to any segment of the community, it seemed to some of the more traditional landowners that their worst fears were about to be realized. The word spread like a hot brushfire through the part of the land-dependent community that had been observing the activities of the restoration groups from a skeptical distance. The documentation provided by the restoration groups was being picked up by regulatory agencies and many people feared these agencies would initiate new and Draconian rules that would make it impossible to make a living from the land. Now a large part of the ranching community began to feel that its very survival was being threatened.

In truth, the personnel of the California Department of Forestry (CDF), the agency in charge of regulating timber operations, had little idea of how to implement such a concept as net zero sedimentation on the naturally unstable ground of the coastal range. But they could not ignore such a strongly worded memorandum. They set up two public meetings to discuss implementation of zero net discharge.

The stated purpose of the second meeting was to form a steering committee to continue discussion of priorities. By the time it convened, emotions were running high. There was a lot of shouting. The ranchers had organized themselves into a bloc of opposition, and in the afternoon the bloc walked out. I feared that efforts to unify the community had come to an end right there. But Richard Harris, a university extension forester who was helping to run the meeting, shot from the hip.

"Wait," he shouted, in a voice loud enough for the people in the lobby to hear. "You can't leave now! You've got too much invested. If you don't want a steering committee, just form an agenda committee. Keep talking to each other, leave the government out!"

"Leave the government out" seemed to be magic words. Cantankerous Anne Smith, a rancher who had never been shy about sharing her critiques of the MRC's strategies, grabbed the hand of Rondal Snodgrass of Sanctuary Forest, by this time a high-profile preservationist, who was sitting next to her. "*We'll* be on the agenda committee!" If the sudden emergence of thesis and antithesis in the newly polarized community had caught me by surprise, it was nothing compared to the startling synthesis that would follow.

The agenda committee had three long and grueling meetings at Anne Smith's home. With the skillful facilitation of Dan Weaver, a retired U.S. Navy officer, the members of this group of eleven—composed of ranchers, two industrial foresters, one dedicated fisheries biologist, and a few of us who came from the newer population—were finally able to hear each other clearly enough to recognize a common basis for communication in our shared concern for the health of the watershed and most particularly in the survival of the native salmon.

The next step was a public meeting under the rubric of the Mattole Watershed Alliance, in April of 1991, which was attended by some two hundred and fifty diverse people, a startling 10-plus percent of the entire resident population.

Thus the Alliance was launched, and it met monthly for two years. Attendance stayed high, a consistent twenty-five to fifty people, and remained broadly representative. The meetings provided a safe arena where the human part of our place could talk to itself about the nonhuman parts and processes that define the conditions of their inhabitation. Anarchism prevailed and the group was never able to institutionalize itself beyond the agreement to reach decisions by consensus, a new and sometimes troubling concept the discussion of which occupied a part of every agenda. Whoever showed up at meetings *was* the Alliance.

However difficult it was to achieve, in consensus the Alliance found a tool that contained a power that surprised everyone. When consensual recommendation from such a broadly representative group was sent to government agencies, those agencies responded.

A memo was initiated by resort owners to recommend the curtailment of sport fishing during the peak of the salmon run. The state Fish and Game Commission, previously experienced by the area's inhabitants as a remote and unapproachable bureaucracy, responded with an unprecedented experimental five-year closure of all recreational fishing in the Mattole from October 1 until January 1 each year, by which time the bulk of the salmon run was past. Resorts could then welcome customers who wanted to fish for the hardier steelhead, from whom they gained most of their annual income anyway. The Humboldt County Department of Public Works instituted a policy of hauling the landslide spoils that periodically closed county roads to stable sites rather than bulldozing them into the nearest watercourse. When the work of the Salmon Group was denied funding by the DFG one year, a letter from the Alliance got it reinstated.

The Alliance also had the effect of creating a forum for the growth of a responsible, inhabitory middle ground, a concept Dan Trower, leader of the Honeydew Volunteer Fire Company, liked to call the radical center. The consensual process assured that no one's ideological toes got trampled; anyone not pleased with the compromises the process often entailed was free to leave the group and pursue other options. (A discussion revolving around a post-fire timber salvage plan by Pacific Lumber, which included a rare on-site tour, never reached consensus. Two environmentalists left the circle and filed suit. The corporate interests felt betrayed and didn't attend the next few meetings.)

As long as the Alliance concerned itself exclusively with salmon, it built a shared history of small successes that explained the loyalty with which people continued to attend the long meetings. It made sense to some to take the next logical step: to develop community standards for logging practices. We were novice swimmers but confident enough by now to dive into the deeper water.

Incredibly, we found that there was no widely agreed upon description of the structure, function, and viable size of old-growth forests, let alone a legal definition, and this became a concern to both environmentalists and the owners of working land whose holdings included some small remnants of old forest that they liked to think of as financial safety nets should a medical emergency arise or the kids need to go away to school. A small subcommittee of environmentalists, ranchland owners, restorationists, and industrial foresters worked hard at developing a broadly acceptable description. The process took a year, but resulted in a clearly and briefly worded document in the form of a letter to Mattole landowners describing the seven most important ecological aspects of old-growth stands in the natural succession of the forest mosaic. It also gently urged landowners to manage their forest land in such a way as to "retain, improve, and enhance" the seven habitat components "to achieve and maintain species richness in the managed and unmanaged forests . . . [and so] improve the health and diversity of the watershed, for now and for the future, for ourselves and for posterity."

To everyone's relief, the alliance as a whole approved the document. But what to do with it? Someone proposed the obvious. Pass the hat to cover mailing expenses and mail it out to the entire resident mailing list maintained by the Mattole Restoration Council.

The Alliance was by now committed to consensus, and somewhere along the line it had managed to twice import "consensus trainers" for lengthy but well-attended workshops. In those sessions, the participants had learned of the power and gravity which resided in any individual's decision to block consensus, that the block is a tool that should only be exercised out of the deep conviction that the impending decision would harm the group as a whole, and not out of personal interest. Blocking power had never before been exercised at previous Alliance meetings; when consensus had not been reached on other thorny issues, they had been deferred for further discussion.

I have never doubted the integrity and conviction of the

two men who blocked the decision to do a broadcast mailing of the graceful letter about old-growth forests. But their action taught me the depth of desperation experienced by resident land managers who feel victimized by the seemingly never-ending battle between popular environmental reformers and the monolithic entanglement of government and corporate power. The rules of consensus the Alliance had adopted required clear articulation of the reason for stopping further discussion. "Some government agency or other will pick this up and use it against us," they said. "And they don't understand our land or our situation."

At the end of the discussion of the letter, on an unseasonally warm day in May of 1993, the Alliance was exhausted. Except for occasional meetings to protect its previous achievements, and occasional sporadic attempts to revive it, the Alliance has yet to recover the vigor, dedication, and moral power of its first two years.

As writer Brenda Peterson tells us, "The new environmentalism is *not* a war, it is a reconciliation and a search for shared territory."[15] Cultural behavior is every bit as mutable, as evolutionary, as any other system. We have discovered in natural systems the cycles of disturbance and recovery. As Thomas Berry points out repeatedly, humans are that aspect of creative evolution that has become self-conscious. We have the ability to create situations and therapeutic strategies that will cause correspondingly self-corrective shifts in cultural norms. We have the capacity to initiate our own cycles of recovery.

The strategy that commands my attention now is to work toward consolidation of the efforts by literally hundreds of North American communities to redefine themselves variously within the constraints and opportunities of their unique living places, as we are trying to do on the Mattole. The biosphere requires of us, I believe, that we do whatever it takes to rediscover ourselves as people of place.

We should not be surprised that our efforts at recovering place-based community proceed by fits and starts. As we awaken from the dream of total dominion, we find ourselves struggling to understand the world as it is. Adapting to that world requires that we understand ourselves as individuals, as groups, and as one species among others—that we learn to live our collective and individual lives on the Earth's own terms. As we do so we discover a sense of time embedded in the slow and cyclical processes of natural succession, a sense of time at odds with our civilized habituation to the ideal of linear progress.

Engaging the lives of wild salmon in a single watershed has created a situation wherein the peoples of our place have begun to experience themselves as functional parts of the place itself. Engaging the lives of any part of the wild in any self-defined natural area will lead to the same experience. We find ourselves reintroduced to our most ancient of teachers of moderation of human behavior—the other species that occupy our particular terrain of interdependence. ("Any animal," a Kuyukon elder once told Richard Nelson, "knows way more than you do.")

A primary benefit of any attempt at environmental restoration is that it creates a situation that allows us to begin to learn from the patterns of the wild around us and within us, the patterns which shaped our mental capacities in the first place, shaped the autonomic processes that maintain our daily functioning all unbidden.

Salmon is a particularly adept teacher. In the two decades since 1978, tens of thousands of people in salmon-bearing watersheds in North America have discovered their love for the vanishing stocks. Salmon is regaining its status as the totem creature of the North Pacific Rim. Salmon, who spend most of their lives hidden from us in the vast oceans, return to instruct us and feed us. They focus our attention on some of the smaller increments of the natural world—the streams that run through our rural homes or beneath our urban structures—at the same time as they instruct us regarding the indivisible relationship of one locale to another and the life lessons to be learned from other species.

In the last ten years, watershed councils and alliances have sprouted up as if from seeds lain dormant for centuries waiting for the right conditions of soil and climate to germinate. The best of these groups are moving toward what writer Donald Snow refers to as "a politics appropriate to place." Snow goes on to describe a strategy of community-based conservation that "fosters the notion that local people can create a base of knowledge sufficient to manage lands, waters, habitat, natural areas, areas to be developed—and that if they can somehow achieve power to do so, they will often (but surely not always) rise to the task."[16]

The task that Snow is delineating might also be described as the process of becoming *indigenous,* a word that at its root means being *of* a place. When we look for models of sustainability in what we know of traditional indigenous cultures, we discover patterns of self-regulation in the form of ritualized practices. Most contemporary Americans understand ritual only in the context of our own (imported) religious traditions; we find it difficult to grasp its relationship to the landscapes we wish to embrace. (For my part, I have been as embarrassed by shallow countercultural and New Age attempts to imitate native American rituals as those Indians who do understand the true functions of these rituals have been angered by them.)

The focus on consensus by place-based groups may contain the elements of a new ritual practice of our own. Consensual decision-making is often misunderstood, both by its practitioners and by its critics, as being either an adjunct or a threat to the power struggles that have come to define institutional democracy. But in its best sense, and if pursued over time, the struggle toward consensus is an attempt to abandon the inequities that inevitably rise from such power struggles. Consensus needs to be understood as the *practice* of community-building in the context of living places. Its appropriate analog is not politics but the processes of natural succession. It is an ongoing collective meditation that allows for conflicting ideologies to gradually be dissolved by a growing sense of mutuality.

A tree growing on a denuded stream bank has no sense of intention, no predetermined goal. But its cooling shade and its binding roots over time have consequence. The stream it shades grows cooler, is slowly scoured to bedrock. When the tree completes its life, it falls into the water to provide nutrients for aquatic insects, which in turn feed salmon, and the salmon feed the carnivores and omnivores at the stream's banks. This pattern is predictable in a general sense, but the particularities are not.

It takes a long time. If the tree is on a river that has become destabilized by human practices upstream, it may be uprooted by floods before its role in recovery has played itself out. Such a flood could be a metaphor for the external forces of history and commerce that continually buffet communities attempting to define themselves. Perhaps the flood and the uprooted tree will have taught some of the nearby humans something of the virtues of patience, humility, and mutuality. Perhaps a group of these people will come down to the water and plant another tree in its place and in the process become entrained, drawn into the slow beauty of the self-healing nature of living places.

EPILOGUE: THE CAPACITY TO BECOME HUMAN

Ironically, as we work to save the salmon,

it may turn out that the salmon save us.

PAUL SCHELL, MAYOR OF SEATTLE

J N ONE ANCIENT LANGUAGE, the word *memory* derives from a word meaning mindful, in another from a word to describe a witness, in yet another it means, at root, to grieve. To witness mindfully is to grieve for what has been lost.

The memory of the salmon themselves remains a mystery that teases human rationality. Biologists like to locate salmon's capacity to remember in the olfactory organs: the fish identify their natal homes by the smell of the waters of their birthplace, we are told, separated out somehow from the infinitude of smells in the planet's oceans. Even as such sensory skill causes me to marvel, I suspect this is too reductionist a description. One has only to watch a school of young salmon moving as if impelled by a single common thought to know that there is something else going on, some mutual mindfulness that resides in the species. I grieve for a quality of mind that seems to have been lost in my own species' evolution.

But perhaps our skills of mutual perception and adaptive response are not lost but only temporarily misplaced in the transient quality of contemporary civilization that philosopher Charlene Spretnak calls modernity. Spretnak describes modernity as a medium that surrounds us as water surrounds fishes, a medium that truncates our native ability to experience life as a multitude of shared memories, both those of our own kind and those of other orders, genera, and species.[1]

When mindful witness becomes collective it gives rise to territory, a place to experience the Earth. As our individual mindful witness is turned purposefully outward, we are transformed; we become part of a piece of the planet's own memory. We find individualism, the holy grail of modernity, not diminished but grown into a mature interpenetration of individualities; we grow larger. Human memory is no longer an isolate experience; it becomes a part of the place's own memory, the whole that promises relief from our unbearable isolation. We grieve when any part of that memory is erased—as it is when another species disappears from our common homes.

From the window of the room where I write I can see on the furthest ridgeline a ten-year-old plantation of native Douglas-fir. The trees are planted among the silvery stumps of other trees that were cut years ago in an attempt to expand the natural prairie for the use of cattle and sheep. Only recently have the new trees grown tall enough so that I can see them above the brushy tangle of coyote brush and poison oak that have occupied the land in the absence of fire or grazing animals. The sight triggers a host of memories each time I glance out that way.

I remember a statement made by an earlier owner of the

land in a public forum about land-use practices. "I'm a rancher," he had said, "I grow grass for a living." A whole philosophy succinctly stated.

I remember that the new trees are just a few of the three hundred thousand planted on converted forestlands by a co-operative program between the MRC, the Soilbankers, and a few northern California mail-order businesses that supported the effort as a responsible mitigation for the paper used in their mass-mailed catalogs. I had been on that site the day some of the employees of one of the companies, Smith and Hawken, had come out to plant a few trees themselves. I remember the spark of pleasure in their urban eyes as they worked alongside the local people.

Out the same window, closer by, I can see just a few of the ancient trees in the Mill Creek Forest, the last uncut grove of significant size in the lower valley of the Mattole. I recall the ten years of effort it took the Mill Creek Watershed Conservancy to turn a $50,000 grant from the state Resources Agency into a convincing argument that the Bureau of Land Management should add the tract to the King Range National Conservation Area at a cost grown to $2.4 million. I recall that in 1992 the management policy of the sixty-thousand-acre KRNCA was changed from "multiple use" to rededicate its lands specifically to the recovery of the Northern spotted owl that is inseparable from the recovery of mature forest complexes. Occasionally I wander in the forest itself and recover some fragment of memory of what the land was like a hundred and fifty years ago.

At the end of a day of work this summer I have sometimes gone down the hill to swim in the healing waters near the mouth of Mill Creek. A new swimming hole has shaped itself there this year, in part because of a small wing dam built by the Salmon Group just upstream of the confluence, in part because of the torrent of debris that poured out of the North Fork of the Mattole, just a few miles upstream, on the flood of New Year's Day 1997. The enlarged delta at the mouth of the North Fork has tweaked the meander of the whole river downstream, filling in most of the deeper, cooler pools. Now the river is beginning to scour new holes in new places. Swimming spots quickly gain names; this one is known by local residents as the Mill Creek Hole.

There are usually a few people swimming or sunbathing at the Mill Creek Hole when I arrive. Some of them will be marveling at the large school of young coho salmon and steelhead gathered in the plume of chilled water pouring out of Mill Creek, waiting for the rains that will break open the berm which blocks their passage to the sea. All summer long, the water in the creek remains fifteen degrees cooler than the overheated river. Some of the people who come here know the history that created this cool refuge for the fish that gather in the heat of the late afternoon. If they don't, I tell them. I can't help myself. The memory is as much a part of who I am as is the growth of my family.

The culvert under the county road through which Mill Creek passes is just visible two hundred yards back up from the swimming hole. It is the same poorly placed culvert that caused Rex Rathbun such anguish twenty years ago, the same one that had created an insurmountable barrier to the migrations of the coho salmon native to Mill Creek when it was built to replace the one that had been washed out in the flood of 1964.

By nature, Rex is impatient with human folly, and it made him mad that such a correctable error had extirpated the Mill Creek salmon run. He has spent his life fixing things, making things work. Rex allowed his anger to inform his intelligence and worked with the fledgling Salmon Group during the 1980s to pull together a cooperative project with the county and the state. A series of check dams of large imported rock was constructed so as to step the level of the streambed back up to something resembling its original gradient; upmigrating salmonids can once again gain passage to their spawning grounds beyond the culvert. The rocks have tumbled into natural configurations as the winter storms have come and gone. Now moss grows on their stable surfaces. Cold pools continue to scour themselves to clean bedrock downstream of the structures; caddis and stone flies hatch in the gravels that accumulate above them. Fifteen- and twenty-year-old alders and willows shade the lower reach of Mill Creek almost entirely, maintaining the cool temperatures provided as the waters run through the old forest a little further upstream.

Through the early eighties, the Salmon Group also maintained its most daunting sustained effort as its members incubated coho salmon and reared them to yearling size for release into the creek. It was daunting because the water flow to rearing pools had to be maintained throughout several particularly fierce winters, when the high waters were laden with silt; at times, two-hour watches had been established around the clock to assure that the water intakes installed in the beds of feeder streams didn't clog. By 1986, a total of nearly twenty-four thousand yearling fish had been released over a period of five years, but state biologists were doubtful that even these numbers were large enough to be significant. During the same period of time, local restoration workers guided California Conservation Corps crews in the modification of fourteen logjams in the lower mile of the creek. Through these efforts and other projects, accessible spawning habitat was increased by 150 percent.

With winter monitoring efforts spread thin across the whole of the riverine watershed, no conclusive proof emerged that the coho restoration effort had resulted in a re-stabilized population. Some small part of the collective community psyche held its breath for twelve years through cycles of flood and drought.

Then, in the summer of 1998, more than a year after coho salmon had been listed as threatened in northern California under the provisions of the Endangered Species Act, the National Marine Fisheries Service contracted a team of biologists to determine the presence or absence of coho in various tributaries of the Mattole. Guided by Salmon Group diver Maureen Roche, the team spent an hour snorkeling in Mill Creek and counted around fifty coho juveniles in three cold pools. The collective psyche has allowed itself a tentative exhalation.

No one will ever know if it was the introduction of juvenile fish into the creeks, or the restoration and maintenance of habitat, or the protection of the ancient forest, or a combination of the three that has resulted in the presence of coho here. No one much cares. Human hands have been applied in ways that resonate with the resilience of the recovery of the wild. I am compelled to tell this story, too, to my newer neighbors. If these stories are not kept alive in the collective memory, the salmon might be allowed to disappear once more.

The Salmon Group has maintained its primary program, the capture and incubation of native king salmon eggs, over eighteen winter seasons. Through cycles of funding as unpredictable as the weather, the group has managed to get its weirs in the water each one of those seasons, still under the guidance of David Simpson and Gary Peterson. I aban-

doned my place in the winter cohort in 1986, to give my time
to the slightly drier work of the Mattole Restoration Council. A second wave of enthusiasts has taken on large parts of
the collective work: Maureen Roche (who introduced un-
derwater monitoring and seems to spend as much time in the
river in all seasons as she does out of it), Ray Lingel, Colum
Coyne, and Ron Lyons (Mattole residents and displaced
fishermen who have taken on much of the annual egg-taking
work), and many others. Nearly half a million young-of-the-
year native salmon have been released back into the river.
Egg-to-fry survival rate has remained high at an average of
over 87 percent, an eightfold increase over what could be expected in a river system so severely degraded.

As we know, the escapement counts decreased from an estimated three thousand in 1980 to a low of some two hundred in 1990–91. In the years since then, the comparative
counts have grown in excruciatingly small—but steady—
annual increments to an estimated one thousand in 1996–
97. The numbers dipped only slightly in the face of the new
El Niño winter of 1997–98. The steady dedication of the
group throughout the difficult eighties in the face of such
ripe opportunities for despair can only be explained by a passion born of love of place, and by the love of salmon carried
by the growing numbers of watershed inhabitants who continue to swell the workforce available to the Salmon Group
and the Restoration Council.

How satisfying and just it would be if the resident effort
could credit its own survival as the determining factor in the
seeming rebound of the stocks. But we cannot do so with
any certainty. "It's too early to say," one worker will tell
you, and this is true. "Too many variables," another will
shrug when embarrassed by over-exuberant praise. This is
also true. Meanwhile the Salmon Group repairs its tattered

weir panels and worn holding tubes, tunes up its single one-ton truck, and readies its raingear for yet another venture into the cold winter waters.

The variables combine into an unsolvable equation, each element of which provides more questions than answers. The indications of recovery have occurred during a period of usually stable weather patterns, which have included at least two seasons of optimal flow conditions in the Mattole River during the salmon's upstream migration. Little-understood cycles of ocean nutrient abundance and a commercial fishery regulated almost out of existence further complicate the equation. Projects in habitat rehabilitation and successes in creating protected refugia have certainly improved the outlook for the natural reproductive success of salmon, but there remains no way to calculate the combined contribution of our human efforts. Small increments of improvement in land-use practices must be intuited rather than quantified. And in a climate of diminishing timber resources, the corporate owners of the headwaters of important tributaries become increasingly aloof to efforts to mount community standards of self-regulation. As the era of the nation-state draws to a close, they have become, in fact, more aggressive. Should they succeed in their insistence on clear-cutting unstable slopes to within yards of the streams that are the mothers of waters, the resultant landslides could destroy all our collective efforts in a single winter.

The Salmon Group has set as its goal the consistent presence of two thousand pairs of king salmon spawners in the river each year, and twenty-five hundred pairs of coho. Should those goals be reached, then—perhaps—the fishers will allow themselves the pleasures of an occasional salmon feast in warm, dry winter homes. In my admittedly biased opinion, if it weren't for the enduring effort of the Salmon Group, there is every likelihood that these native stocks of salmon would have been lost forever.

I climb into my pickup to visit my friend Rondal, who lives at the opposite end of the watershed, near its headwaters. As I drive the length of the river's course, I recall driving this road weekly during my involvement in generating *Elements of Recovery,* more than ten years ago. For the first few months of that two-year project, I had used the trip to memorize the names and watershed configurations of every tributary stream I passed. In the map in my mind, the names had the shape of empty polygons demanding to be filled. As the months grew into years, the creek names grew into pictures of live drainages: their patterns of vegetation, their networks of roads, their conditions of disturbance and recovery, their friendliness to salmon.

As I drive the same road now, those patterns have deepened, grown richer and more detailed, so detailed that they are beyond the capacities of a single mind to encompass. The pictures in my mind are linked to the patterns of experience and intimacy that reside in the minds of the inhabitants of all the tributary streams I pass. I note a peculiar sense of expansion when I pass near the homes of people with whom I have worked most closely over the years. Their mental landscapes are part of mine, and mine of theirs: our memories are connected by the patterns of the landscape, connected by the salmon that run through them.

The Mattole Restoration Council, too, has been enlivened by second and third waves of people who continue to evoke an ever more detailed picture of a common home. Seth Zuckerman has grown into an able chairman of the MRC board of directors while continuing to hone his skills as a journalist. The little office above the community center has become an overflowing resource center, thanks to the efforts of Mickey Dulas, MRC program manager for three years now. The resource center is available to anyone who walks through the door; the telephone rings dozens of times each workday with requests for information or assistance. Ali Freedlund, already a busy mother of two school-age children, reads each of the growing number of industrial timber harvest plans and translates their technical jargon for the benefit of concerned neighbors. There are often one or more young people in the office, new graduates of distant universities whose idealism has somehow remained intact. One such person is Jeremy Wheeler, who for a year has been entering the information from two decades of hand-drawn maps into a sophisticated Geographic Information Systems computer program. Another is Drew Barber, an environmental education graduate who is assuming the role of liaison with the local school district.

The growing body of work stories and research and the ever more richly crowded maps might have gathered dust in government basements as lifeless files, or been used to maintain the mystification required for the continued dominance of "expert" management from centralized locations. Instead they have been shared with the people who can embody them in daily behavior.

> I arrive in the headwaters of the river with half an hour to spare. I pull off the road a mile upstream of the trapping site where this story began. The names of some of the places have changed, and other, more accommodating trapping sites have been located for the Salmon Group's winter work. The place that was called the Dump Hole in 1982 is now known by the locals who swim there as Stanley Creek

Falls. Stevie has died more than ten years ago. His passing caused a shock wave of self-recognition in the community of which he was a part. The memory of his service is expressed in periodic community work parties that keep the river and road clean of trash and debris.

The place where I park my truck is on the edge of the Sanctuary Forest, grown now to a formerly unimaginable thirty-four hundred acres. Its management is a creative collaboration between the land trust and state and federal agencies. Around its edges, experiments in restorative forestry are growing on privately held lands. Patterns of mutuality flow out of the wild center to empower a community engaged in envisioning a sustainable future.

I want to see the river. It is late summer and the flows are as low as they will get this year. I walk down and dip in my hand to test the temperature. The water is cold, cold enough to sustain the darting flashes I know are juvenile salmon. The waterway is enclosed in an embrace of exuberant vegetation; everywhere the light is dappled and the air filled with the sweetness of ozone where the river crashes over bedrock extrusions. Where the water slows to flow over long reaches of gravel it is so clear as to seem invisible. Fifteen years ago, when I walked this same reach, a kick of my rubber boot would dislodge enough silt to obscure the bottom. Today I reach down and collect a handful of small cobbles of just the size preferred by king salmon for burying their eggs. When I drop the rocks back into the river, fine sediments are washed away as individual particles that glint and sparkle where light hits the water.

I walk by the river for half an hour. I pass a few of the streambank stabilization structures built of native stone by Richard Gienger and his crews more than fifteen years ago, so carefully placed that nearly all of them have survived several flood winters in their original configuration. Wet mosses thrive on the rocks; salmonberry and five-fingered ferns grow from the interstices that have captured the soils carried by flood waters. The structures appear to be at the same time natural parts of the living stream and expressions of human culture as evocative as the stones of ancient cathedrals.

I pass other structures, part of a project finished only this year by a new generation of workers under the direction of Gary Peterson. These have a different function. They are meant to hold in place the fallen trees and rootwads so essential to the function of a healthy aquatic ecosystem, and they represent the recognition that too much of the large wood had been removed from the riparian corridor—swept out to sea by floods, or taken out for its economic value, or purposely removed because of earlier theories of streambank health that were driven by an esthetic of tidiness rather than by ecological wisdom. The structures combine wind-felled trees, butt sections of ancient redwoods left behind by loggers years ago, and large rock, all cabled and bolted and anchored so that they will remain in place until the next generation of riparian trees falls into the river at the end of their lives.

The glint of bright cable and nuts at the end of threaded rod will dull in time, be hidden by the smaller debris the structures will capture in future winters. So freshly placed, some of them have a harsh or whimsical appearance reminiscent of modernist art. I am especially delighted by one—a boulder too large to have been carried there by the most violent flood bolted atop an old tree bole, the other end of which is buried in the streambank. It draws the eye like an artfully made puzzle in a Zen garden. By this time next year, the river will have engaged in its part of this artistic collaboration be-

tween people and nature, and the appearance of the structure will be changed—which leads me to the thought that as
we become part of the place's own memory, our grief for
what is lost may become a vision of what might be regained.

The tendency of environmental activists has been to
organize their strategies in reaction and resistance to what
we know is wrong. This is predictable, since what is wrong is
so large and so well organized that such resistance sometimes seems to occupy every erg of available human energy.
Our daily lives become defined by our responses to the powerful mechanisms of growth, development, and consumer-
ism on a global scale. These mechanisms are usually able to
absorb our agitation as part of the cost of doing business. We
become part of the machinery, one step removed. Thus the
environmental movement has become, as Peter Berg has
pointed out, a part of the mainstream judicial system.

When we begin to focus on what might be right—the appropriate contexts, scales, and economies in which human
communities might immerse themselves in local expressions
of the planet—we find ourselves creating new language. As
a species, we have become a population of refugees, long-
ing for homes we remember only faintly, as we remember
dreams. The process of reconstructing and immersing ourselves in our own specific places at times resembles the effort
to recreate the memory of a victim of amnesia.

As we hear large centralized agencies—institutionally in-
capable of yielding much of their hard-won dominance—
use phrases like "watershed management," "bioregional
governance," and "ecosystem management," it can appear as
if we may simply be creating "a new pasture of jargon for
our adversaries to graze on," as a friend put it recently. It
doesn't much matter what we call such initiatives. Whether

identified as regional self-regulation, community-based conservation, reinhabitation, or ecocultural restoration, they all
have one thing in common. If community-based efforts to recover the sources of security and identity in place are to succeed, then the communities must by definition determine
their own priorities. New language, if it is truly new or radical (that is, "from the root"), cannot be co-opted without
changing the co-opter in some measure. To a certain degree
(and it is a measure of our intelligence to be aware to *what*
degree), the indicator of our success is not the avoidance of
co-optation but to have designed strategies that cannot be co-
opted without a fundamental change on the part of the larger
socioeconomic system.

Journalist Phillip Johnson asks, "Can an economy respect
a watershed without the watershed and its residents having a
real status in the economy? There is no name for an economy
that has the watershed as a basic unit; contemplating that
question might open up a whole new avenue of thought."[2]
Pursuing that thought, David Simpson will tell you that it
is unethical to work at dismantling a destructive economy
without at the same time working to build an alternative
one, regionally centered, that provides displaced workers
with a way to remain at work in the places they love.

To that end, David has led the board of directors of the Institute for Sustainable Forestry, based in nearby Redway,
California, for the last four years.[3] The institute has designed
a program of certification for lumber produced in a way that
enhances the health of the forests and the rivers that run
through them. Similar regional strategies have united into an
international certification program under the label "Smart
Wood," to provide consumers with the choice of building
supplies that do not come from ecosystems that are treated
as expendable. The organization is at the same time working

to create a model for a decentralized watershed-based economy based on the judicious use of California hardwoods, gorgeous woods that are currently clear-cut for pulp.

In a similar vein, agronomist Wes Jackson advocates a university curriculum he calls Homecoming, regionally centered and dedicated to the recovery of the diverse and exuberant cultures of place:

We must give standing to the new pioneers, the homecomers bent on the most important work of the next century—a massive salvage operation to save the vulnerable but necessary pieces of nature and culture and to keep the good and artful examples before us. It is time for a new breed of artists to enter front and center, for *the point of art, after all, is to connect.* This is the homecomer I have in mind: the scientist, the accountant who converses with nature, a true artist devoted to the building of agriculture and culture to match the scenery presented to those first European eyes. [Emphasis added.]*

From my perspective, we might best begin earlier in the students' lives. For each of fifteen consecutive years, Gary Peterson and Maureen Roche have carried into the elementary schools in the Mattole watershed a few fertilized native salmon eggs that have grown into fish before the students' eyes in glass-sided incubators. For eighteen years, it has been these kids who have bucketed the legions of native salmon juveniles back to their home in the wild. The students have come to think of this as normal behavior, predictable, a chance to get out of the classroom. In an outdoor mural painted by students, among the humans beside the bank of a river some are carrying fishing rods, some are holding white plastic buckets full of young salmon.

With the Restoration Council as regional coordinator, the local school district is adopting a K–12 curriculum called

Adopt-a-Watershed. The program uses the patterns of the lands and waters of the students' own home place as primary instructors in the sciences of biology, ecology, and geology. The kids will return to the same location each year, studying bugs one year, birds the next, eventually delving into more complex studies of hydrological and ecological relationships. They will build their own phenological calendars and databases. They will take part in environmental restoration projects where practical. Who can anticipate the effects of learning the sciences through direct engagement with the world right outside the classroom window rather than from textbooks that fail to locate that study in unique places?

I walk in a world I have come to understand as mutable, ever-changing. My walk on the next morning carries me into streaming fog blowing off the Pacific into my face. The chill of it shortens my planned route and makes me wonder just how wide that line on the map that divides water from land should be.

The rolling hills around me seem still, but I know that they are not. All the land within my view is called by geologists an accretionary prism. In plainer language, the seemingly solid ground under my feet is made of rubble scraped off the Gorda plate as it dives beneath the North American plate. Such knowledge is occasionally enlivened by an adrenal rush that is a response to the rumble and roll of the earth, or by a series of sharp jolts that knocks the jars off the shelves in my home. It is the mountains around me rearranging themselves.

After a while, the movement of mountains rearranges the mind. I find in myself a new fluidity of response, a diminished sense of attachment, a more comfortable sense of humility. I am a different person than I was when I arrived in this valley. I may not be alone.

I have taken this same walk repeatedly for nearly twenty years. In one place along the way I can see the flow of the river six hundred feet below. When I first came here, the river flowed on the far side of the floodplain; now it eats at the bank closest to my feet. It will move again. Young trees emerging from impenetrable brush have now grown large enough to shade the viney brambles and poison oak. I have removed some of the lower limbs to reduce fire danger and to encourage the trees to grow straighter. Now a part of my walk takes me through their shade. I am beginning to become conversant with the landscape and the conversation is reciprocal.

It is early autumn now. Soon the salmon will arrive to mill offshore, to feast and be feasted upon as they wait for the berm that blocks their access to the river to be broken by the first rains. There is a bluff overlooking the confluence of the river with the sea. When the berm breaks, I will go up there and watch the murky brown waters of the river pour into the sea. I will know that there are salmon beating upstream against the current, though I won't be able to see them. If this year is like the last few years, there will be other people there. They will come and go all day. No formulist will have called them there. Some will chatter excitedly, comparing the placement of this year's opening of the bar with last year's or speculating about the relative ferocity of the coming winter. Others will stand or sit quietly for a while and then go back to whatever tasks the coming of winter requires; I won't know what is passing through their minds.

For my part, I will be thinking about what salmon are trying to teach us. That there is a way for us humans to be, just as there is a way for salmon to be. That we are related by virtue of the places to which we choose to return.

Claude Levi-Strauss has observed, "In a world where diversity exceeds our mental capacity nothing is impossible in

The epigraph on p. vii is from Tom Jay's essay "Homecoming," in Reaching Home, with additional essays by Brad Matsen and photographs by Natalie Fobes (Anchorage, Alaska: Alaska Northwest Books, 1994).

1 · IN SALMON'S WATER

1 This temptation seems to be a regional institution. See Alfred Kroeber and Samuel Barrett, "Fishing Among the Indians of Northwest California" (University of California Anthropological Records 21:1 [1960]), an encyclopedic approach to indigenous fishing technology, which indicates a more or less even split between using weirs to direct salmon to a fishing platform (only functional when manned by a spear or net fisher) or to a pen checked periodically.

2 See Ferris Neave (Canadian Fisheries Research Board, 1958), quoted in Anthony Netboy's Salmon, the World's Most Harassed Fish (London: A. Deutsch, 1980).

3 Kroeber's work in physical and cultural anthropology among indigenous people of California is legend. See his monumental Handbook of the Indians of California, Bulletin 78 of the Bureau of American Ethnology of the Smithsonian Institution (Washington, D.C.: U.S. Govern-

ment Printing Office, 1925). My copy is a reprint by Dover Publications, 1976.

4 See the work of Erna Gunther, the great ethnobotanist of the Pacific Northwest, especially "A Further Analysis of the First Salmon Ceremony," in University of Washington Publications in Anthropology 2:5 (Seattle: University of Washington Press, 1928).

5 Researcher Deborah Carver has related Yurok "myths" of land formation and the destruction and dispersal of peoples as evidence of a massive earthquake on the Cascadian subduction zone within tribal memory. More recent studies have dated the last massive movement of the Cascadian subduction zone as occurring on January 26, 1700.

2 · GHOSTS & PRESENCES

1 Willa Nehlson, J. E. Williams, and J. A. Lichatowich, "Pacific Salmon at the Crossroads: Stocks at Risk from California, Oregon, Idaho, and Washington," *Fisheries* 16:2 (1991).

2 See R. J. Childerhose and Marj Trim, *Pacific Salmon* (Seattle: University of Seattle Press, 1979). The only fault I can find with this beautiful book is that its sources are not noted. I have not sought further for the author of this research.

3 Terry Roelofs, personal communication.

3 · MOUNTAINS IN MOTION

I owe the epigraph to this chapter to Danny Hagen, a proactive geologist who teaches people how to build and maintain roads. This version of a concept he often slips into his lectures was caught by Seth Zuckerman in "Heavy Equipment and Hotshot Operators for Watershed Restoration," in Whole Earth, *summer 1998.*

1 Robert N. Coats, "The Road to Erosion," *Environment* 20:1 (January/February 1978).

2 Gladys Ayer Nomland, "Sinkyone Notes," University of California Publications in American Archaeology and Ethnology 36:2 (Berkeley, California: University of California, 1935).

4 · RITES OF REGULATION

The epigraph to this chapter, attributed to Sioux elder Brave Buffalo, comes from William Least-Heat Moon's PrairyEarth *(Boston: Houghton Mifflin, 1991).*

1 A reproduction of this painting may be found in Joseph Campbell's *The Way of the Animal Powers* (San Francisco: Harper and Row, 1983), 205.

2 T. T. Waterman and A. L. Kroeber, "The Kepel Fish Dam," University of California Publications in Archaeology and Ethnology 35:6 (Berkeley, California: University of California, 1938), 49–80.

3 Lucy Thompson, *To the American Indian* (Berkeley, California: Heyday Books, 1991), 178.

4 Sean L. Swezey and Robert F. Heizer, "Ritual Management of Salmonid Fish Resources in California," *Journal of California Anthropology* 4:1 (1977).

5 Ibid.

6 Thompson, *To the American Indian,* 185.

7 Karuk Tribe of California, "Karuk Module for the Main Stem Salmon River Watershed Analysis: Scoping of Tribal Issues for Karuk Aboriginal Territory," USDA Forest Service, Yreka, California, 25 June 1996.

8 The Bunnel quotation here is from *Planetedge,* a series of posters self-published and distributed by Peter Berg in 1969. Berg later founded the Planet Drum Foundation and has maintained an essential role in the development of bioregional thinking.

5 · THE CLIENTS OF SCIENCE

1 Anthony Netboy, *Salmon, the World's Most Harassed Fish* (London: A. Deutsch, 1980). In 1798, the Upper Locks and Canals Company built a sixteen-foot-high dam across the Connecticut River, blocking salmon migration. Later other dams rose. In 1814, Dr. Samuel Latham Mitchell reported in *Fishes of New York* that New York City could no longer obtain its salmon from the Connecticut. When a solitary stray turned up in a fisherman's net near Old Saybrook, Connecticut, in 1872, at first no one could identify it.

By 1840, the Merrimack and Connecticut Rivers were the primary sources of power for two-thirds of the twelve hundred textile mills in the United States. Salmon continued to use the Merrimack in ever-decreasing numbers until 1847, when Francis C. Lowell, promoter of the power loom, built a mill near Lawrence, Massachusetts, that blocked upstream migration and extirpated the run within a dozen years. Henry David Thoreau complained about the depopulation of the rivers in *A Week on the Concord and Merrimack Rivers*, published in 1839.

By 1870 there were only seven rivers—all in Maine—that supported natural runs of Atlantic salmon on the whole of the east coast of the United States.

2 Seth Green and R. B. Roosevelt, *Fish Hatching and Fish Catching* (Rochester, New York: Union and Advertiser Co.'s Book and Job Print, 1879), quoted in Daniel L. Bottom, "To Till the Waters: A History of Ideas in Fisheries Conservation," in *Pacific Salmon and Their Ecosystems* (New York: Chapman and Hall, 1997).

3 Arthur F. McEvoy, *The Fisherman's Problem: Ecology and Law in the California Fisheries, 1850–1980* (London: Cambridge University Press, 1986).

4 Ibid.

5 See Donald Worster, *Nature's Economy: The Roots of Ecology* (San Francisco: Sierra Club Books, 1977). Although the German biologist Ernst Haeckel had introduced the idea of an interdisciplinary science that would devote itself to the study of the interrelationships of organisms in his 1866 book *Oecologie,* the word did not gain public currency (and its modern spelling) until the International Botanical Congress of 1893.

6 Livingston Stone, as quoted in Joel W. Hedgpeth, "Livingston Stone and Fish Culture in California," in *California Fish and Game* 20:3 (1940): 126–48.

7 McEvoy, *The Fisherman's Problem.*

8 Stone's ambitions weren't limited to North America. In the 1890s, Sacramento River chinook salmon eggs were shipped to New Zealand, where they were successfully hatched out and introduced into Southern Hemisphere streams for the first time. The few fish adapted and proliferated to numbers large enough to support a commercial fishery. Later introductions by other enthusiasts produced viable fisheries elsewhere in the Southern Hemisphere, in Chile and Australia. Much later, chinook salmon were also successfully introduced into the Great Lakes. (Hedgpeth, "Livingston Stone.")

9 Hedgpeth notes that it was the lobbying of the commercial striped bass fishery that eventually lead to the closure of gillnetting on the Sacramento River. (Ibid.)

10 Ibid.

11 U.S. Fish Commission Bulletin No. 16 (1896): "A report upon salmon investigations in the headwaters of the Columbia together with notes

upon the fishes observed in that state in 1894 and 1895," quoted in Hedgpeth, "Livingston Stone" without further attribution, but Hedgpeth notes that both Evermann's and Stone's observations were included in the report.

12 McEvoy, *The Fisherman's Problem.*

13 Hedgpeth, "Livingston Stone."

14 D. F. Hobbs, "Natural reproduction of quinnat salmon, brown, and rainbow trouts in certain waters of New Zealand," New Zealand Marine Department Fisheries Bulletin No. 6, quoted in Hedgpeth, ibid.

15 See William K. Kier, "California Hatcheries: They've Gone About as Fer as They Can Go!" in *California's Salmon and Steelhead: The Struggle to Restore an Imperiled Resource* (Berkeley, California: University of California Press, 1991).

16 See Joseph Cone and Sandy Ridlington, eds., *The Northwest Salmon Crisis: A Documentary History* (Covallis, Oregon: Oregon State University Press, 1996). Bill Bakke and Joseph Cone quote J. McDonald, "The Stock Concept and Its Application to British Columbia Fisheries, *Canadian Journal of Fisheries and Aquatic Science* 38, in a commentary on pp. 46–50. This volume by Cone and Ridlington is an indispensable reference which repeatedly demonstrates not only that the crisis in salmon population is more than a hundred years old but that the crisis has been forcefully articulated by well-informed voices from every sector throughout that period.

17 Willis H. Rich, "Local Populations and Migration in Relation to the Conservation of Pacific Salmon in the Western States and Alaska," in *The Migration and Conservation of Salmon*, publication No. 8, American Association for the Advancement of Science (Lancaster, Pennsylvania: Science Press, 1939), quoted in Cone and Ridlington, *The Northwest Salmon Crisis.*

I had the good fortune to meet Dr. Rich and spend a few hours with him during his retirement in Marin County, California. Rich was the first person to bring to my attention the large damages that centralized hatcheries can wreak on the natural reproductive strategies of wild salmon. In retirement, he continued to feel the frustration of a superb scientist whose observations are ignored as inconvenient by policy makers. Our meeting took place, serendipitously, during the time that we were trying to understand if our localized hatchbox strategies would hold up under the scrutiny of the best science. Willis had been a witness to the blinking out of many discrete salmon populations during the thirty years since he had published his paper on the home stream theory. He suffered the extirpations with a particularly exquisite pain. At the time of our interview I was unaware of the seminal role Rich had played in American fisheries science, and didn't know enough to ask him for a letter of support. Nevertheless, the felt depth of his enthusiasm for our project did a lot to prop up my own sense of mission during the difficult year that followed.

18 Clifford Geertz, *The Interpretation of Cultures* (New York: Basic Books, 1973).

19 Bottom, "To Till the Waters."

20 Richard White, *The Organic Machine: The Remaking of the Columbia River* (New York: Hill and Wang, 1995).

6 · AT THE HEART OF CREATION

1 See William G. Pearcy, *Ocean Ecology of North Pacific Salmonids* (Seattle: University of Washington Press, 1992). Also see C. Groot and L. Margolis, *Pacific Salmon Life Histories* (Vancouver, British Columbia: University of British Columbia Press, 1991).

2 Nehlson, along with J. E. Williams and Jim Lichatowich, led the research that resulted in the publication by the American Fisheries Society in 1991 of "Pacific Salmon at the Crossroads: Stocks at Risk from California, Oregon, Idaho, and Washington," *Fisheries* 16:2 (1991). This paper demonstrated the precipitous decline of salmon in the continental United States so effectively that it raised public and governmental concern for the situation by a quantum leap. The quote in text here is from Chapter 8 of Ecotrust/Interterrain Pacific's excellent sourcebook *The Rain Forests of Home: Profile of a North American Bioregion*, published by Island Press in 1996.

3 G. W. Hewes, as quoted by Alfred Kroeber and Samuel Barrett in "Fishing Among the Indians of Northwest California," University of California Anthropological Records 21:1 (1960).

4 David Abram, "Thami Valley, Eastern Nepal, May 7–9, 1981" (Silverton, Colorado: Way of the Mountain Learning Center, 1983).

7 · IN PLACE

1 David Simpson, "Dark Nights and High Water on the Mattole," *Siskiyou Journal* 29 (April/May 1987).

2 T. K. Clark, *Regional History of Petrolia and the Mattole Valley* (Eureka, California: Miller Press, 1983).

3 Peter Berg and Raymond Dasmann, "Reinhabiting California," *The Ecologist* 7:10 (December 1977): 399–401; reprinted in *Reinhabiting a Separate Country: A Bioregional Anthology of Northern California,* ed. Peter Berg (San Francisco: Planet Drum Foundation, 1978).

9 · THE WATERSHED

1 Mattole Watershed Salmon Support Group, *Five-Year Management Plan for Salmon Stock Rescue Operations, 1995–96 through 1999–2000,* amended and approved version, November 1995 (available from the Mattole Salmon Group, Box 188, Petrolia, CA 95558). In this document, the most detailed compendium available of Salmon Group activities since 1980, the earliest practical time for withdrawal of population enhancement measures is at such a time that breeding populations entering the river (escapement) average 25 percent of historic levels (1,250 pairs chinook and 500 pairs coho) and sink no lower than 10 percent (500 chinook and 200 coho). At the time of writing (spawning year 1997–98), annual numbers were approaching the minimum level, but had not yet reached the "average" for even one year.

2 The meeting was convened under the Council Madrone, the largest single madrone tree in the world, registered as such by the American Forestry Association. Local lore has it that this is the place where indigenous peoples once met to council.

3 Mattole Restoration Council, *Mattole Restoration Newsletter,* No. 1 (Whitethorn, California: MRC, October 1983). The Council's address as of the publication date of this book is Box 160, Petrolia, CA 95558; e-mail address is mrc@northcoast.com.

4 Paul Shepard, "Place in American Culture," in his book *Traces of an Omnivore* (Washington, D.C.: Island Press, 1996).

5 Michael McGinnis, work in progress.

10 · SUBSTANTIAL & GENUINE VIRTUE

1 The practice of indenturement of Indians by whites was commonplace during the short and brutal conquest of northwest California, as was intermarriage. Indenturement was in fact legalized in California be-

tween 1850 and 1863, under a law entitled "An Act for the Governance and Protection of Indians." It was common practice for Euro-American raiding parties to capture women and children and enslave them. Under the law, this practice could be legalized through the simple expedient of registering the name of the captured native at the county assessor's office. Terms of indenturement ranged from ten to twenty-five years. Jack Norton, in *Genocide in Northwest California,* lists seventy such registrations in Humboldt County, California, between 1860 and 1863. (Our own A. A. Hadley registered two names during this period, and it is easy to imagine that many white settlers may never have bothered with legalizing what was a common practice, given that such registration would require a two-day journey to the county seat in Eureka.) Norton quotes Robert Heizer's estimate in *The Destruction of California Indians* (Santa Barbara, California, and Salt Lake City, Utah: Peregrine Smith, Inc., 1974) that about ten thousand natives were enslaved during this period.

2 T. K. Clark, *Regional History of Petrolia and the Mattole Valley* (Eureka, California: Miller Press, 1983).

3 Anne Matthews, *Where the Buffalo Roam* (New York: Grove Weidenfeld, 1992).

4 L. K. Wood, *The Discovery of Humboldt Bay* (Eureka, California: Society of California Pioneers, 1932). For more on the history of the region, see also Mary Siler Anderson, *Backwoods Chronicles: A History of Southern Humboldt, 1849–1920* (Redway, California: SoHumCo Press, 1985); Dr. Loon, "Tusk Shell Gold Dollar Pulp Note Weed: Four Principles of Economy in the Six Rivers/Humboldt Bay Region," in *Reinhabiting a Separate Country: A Bioregional Anthology of Northern California,* ed. Peter Berg (San Francisco: Planet Drum Foundation, 1978); and Neb Roscoe, *Heydays in Mattole* (Mckinleyville, California: Illiana Limited, 1996).

5 Donald Worster, *The Wealth of Nature: Environmental History and the Ecological Imagination* (New York: Oxford University Press, 1993), p. 98.

6 John Locke, "An Essay Concerning the True Original Extent and End of Government," in *Britannica Great Books,* vol. 35 (Chicago: 1952).

7 Thomas Jefferson, *Notes on the State of Virginia* (New York: Harper Torchbooks, 1964).

8 See Jack Norton, *Genocide in Northwest California* (San Francisco: The Indian Historical Press, 1979).

9 Locke, "The True Original Extent and End of Government."

10 Rebecca Solnit, *Savage Dreams: A Journey into the Hidden Wars of the American West* (San Francisco: Sierra Club Books, 1994).

11 Quoted by Stephen Bodio in "Struck with Consequence," *Northern Lights,* fall 1994.

12 The appointment of Bruce Babbitt as U.S. Secretary of the Interior in 1992, along with the emergence of a new generation of field scientists and area managers, signaled a dramatic shift in the relationship between the resident Mattole restoration groups and federal land managers. As I write, the rule of the day is one of proactive communication and cooperative planning. Ed Hastey, California director of the Bureau of Land Management, must also be given credit as one of the most farsighted proponents and practitioners of this reform from the top.

13 Demographic information from Seth Zuckerman, "Social and Ecological Prospects for Second-Growth Forestry in the Mattole Valley (Humboldt County, California)," Master's Project, Energy and Resources Group, (Berkeley, California: University of California, 1990).

14 Wallace Stegner, *The American West as Living Space* (Ann Arbor, Michigan: University of Michigan Press, 1987).

15 Brenda Peterson, interviewed in *Bloomsbury Review,* September/October 1996.

16 Donald Snow, "A Politics Appropriate to Place," in *Connotations* (the journal of the Island Institute, Sitka, Alaska).

EPILOGUE: THE CAPACITY TO BECOME HUMAN

Paul Schell's remark, used as the epigraph to this chapter, was quoted by Timothy Egan, "Bid To Save Fish Puts West on Notice," New York Times, *27 February 1998.*

1 Charlene Spretnak, *The Resurgence of the Real: Body, Nature, and Place in a Hypermodern World* (Reading, Massachusetts: Addison-Wesley, 1997).

2 Phillip Johnson, reviewing Paul Hawken's *The Ecology of Commerce* in *Amicus,* summer 1994.

3 David Simpson and Jane Lapiner have also recognized from the first that song and dance and theater are powerful iterations of social transformation. Both come from a theatrical background—Jane as a tal-

ented dancer and choreographer, David as a comic actor and a writer of plays and songs. Together, David writing and Jane directing, they produced the musical comedy *Queen Salmon* in the late 1980s. A troupe of actors and musicians, gathered mostly from among experienced restoration workers, toured the play throughout California and the Pacific Northwest before enthusiastic audiences, which most effectively carried the message of the Mattole restoration effort to a wider public.

4 Wes Jackson, *Becoming Native to This Place* (Washington, D.C.: Counterpoint, 1996).

5 Claude Levi-Strauss, *The Savage Mind* (Chicago: University of Chicago Press, 1966).